RECONSTRUCTING REALITY
IN THE COURTROOM

A Volume in the
Crime, Law, and Deviance
Series

RECONSTRUCTING REALITY
IN THE COURTROOM

Justice and Judgment
in American Culture

W. Lance Bennett
and Martha S. Feldman

Rutgers University Press / New Brunswick

First paperback edition, 1984
Second printing, cloth edition, 1984

Library of Congress Cataloging in Publication Data

Bennett, W. Lance.
    Reconstructing reality in the courtroom.

    (Crime, law, and deviance)
    Includes bibliographical references and index.
    1. Criminal procedure—United States.
2. Forensic oratory. 3. Trial practice—United
States. I. Feldman, Martha S., 1953–
II. Title. III. Series.
KF9656.B46   345.73'05   81–5125
ISBN 0–8135–0922-X   347.3055   AACR2
ISBN 0–8135–1078-3 (pbk)

Contents

PART IV. IMPLICATIONS FOR A THEORY
OF TRIAL JUSTICE

Preface

This book is about how stories of the sort people tell in everyday life help to organize the information presented in criminal trials so that it can be evaluated by jurors. Our theory shows how ordinary means of telling and interpreting stories are used in trials to assess the credibility of competing claims. This perspective views the formal rules of the court as ritual that facilitates the presentation of a case but does not dictate its interpretation. In other words, the formal procedures limit the information that will be perceived as relevant to a story, but within the range of admissible information, the actual presentation and interpretation of cases depend primarily on the storytelling and story-hearing abilities of the courtroom actors (i.e., judge, jurors, defense, prosecutor, witnesses). The use of stories to reconstruct the evidence in cases casts doubt on the common belief about justice as a mechanical and objective process.

Shared perceptions of and experiences with justice in a system like this depend on the ability to tell stories equally well and the chance to share the experiences necessary to understand legal accounts clearly. In a society with many subcultures some groups tell stories differently from others, and some groups are not familiar with the experiences of others. Bias in trial justice is not a surprising result of this means of presenting and deciding legal issues.

We thank Julia Ball, Sharon Clarke, and Mary Pierce for their help in typing the manuscript and for providing editorial comments. For reading the manuscript and contributing to our thinking we thank Jonathan D. Casper, Murray Edelman, Elisabeth Hansot, Julie Harrison, Robert E. Lane, James G. March, JoAnne Martin, and Stuart Scheingold. For supporting the authors during the years it took to complete the book, we thank the Graduate School Research Fund of the University of Washington, the Department of Political Science at Stanford University, the Organizations Research Training Program at Stanford University, and the Brookings Institution. We thank Marlie Wasserman for exercising her editorial judgment in ways that have produced a better book. Finally, we thank the many courtroom actors without whom we could not have pursued this research.

PART I
JUSTICE AS AN EVERYDAY PROCESS

Chapter 1

Storytelling in the Courtroom

The question to be explored in these pages is a deceptively simple one: how is justice done by ordinary people in criminal trials? Formal justice processes like the criminal trial require the participation of average citizens who have no formal legal training. As witnesses who introduce evidence, as jurors who evaluate evidence and interpret it within the law, as defendants who must understand the case against them if they are to contribute to their own defense—even as spectators who follow cases and draw conclusions about the fairness of the justice system—these untrained citizens all play a part in the trial process.

If trials make sense to untrained participants, there must be some implicit framework of social judgment that people bring into the courtroom from everyday life. Such a framework would have to be shared by citizen participants and legal professionals alike. Even lawyers and judges who receive formal legal training must rely on some commonsense means of presenting legal issues and cases in ways that make sense to jurors, witnesses, defendants, and spectators.

Our search for the underlying basis of justice and judgment in American criminal trials has produced an interesting conclusion: the criminal trial is organized around storytelling. Although our analysis is based on American case studies, it is clear that there are applications to other justice systems. For example, a number of other societies (England being the most obvious) also employ storytelling in legal judgment. Our analysis of American trials illustrates how an underlying storytelling process can be detected, described, and connected to the formal justice procedures that are unique to a particular society. Even

[3]

when storytelling is not the underlying basis of legal judgment in a society, there is another generalization that can be drawn from the American case: legal judgment involves more than a set of formal procedures for resolving disputes in a society. Formal justice procedures (rules of evidence, uses of case law or opinions, etc.) must engage some parallel form of social judgment that anchors legal questions in everyday understandings. In societies that don't rely on storytelling, the everyday bases of social judgment include forms that range from religious beliefs to somatic reactions to the behaviors of defendants and witnesses. Thus the American case both illustrates the importance of everyday judgment practices in the justice process and shows how a particular everyday judgment and communications device, the story, fits into a formal scheme of legal judgment.

The story is an everyday form of communication that enables a diverse cast of courtroom characters to follow the development of a case and reason about the issues in it. Despite the maze of legal jargon, lawyers' mysterious tactics, and obscure court procedures, any criminal case can be reduced to the simple form of a story. Through the use of broadly shared techniques of telling and interpreting stories, the actors in a trial present, organize, and analyze the evidence that bears on the alleged illegal activity.

The significance of stories in the trial justice process can be summarized as follows: in order to understand, take part in, and communicate about criminal trials, people transform the evidence introduced in trials into stories about the alleged criminal activities. The structural features of stories make it possible to perform various tests and comparisons that correspond to the official legal criteria for evaluating evidence (objectivity, reasonable doubt, and so on). The resulting interpretation of the action in a story can be judged according to the law that applies to the case.

If the importance of storytelling in the justice process can be demonstrated, several of the mysteries surrounding criminal trials can be cleared up. First and most obviously, the storytelling perspective answers the question of how jurors actually organize and analyze the vast amounts of information involved in making a legal judgment. Stories are systematic means of storing, bringing up to date, rearranging, comparing, testing, and interpreting available information about social behavior. As witnesses deliver testimony bearing on alleged illegal behavior, a juror operates much like someone reading a detective novel or watching a mystery movie replete with multiple points of view, subplots, time lapses, missing information, and ambiguous clues.

Stories also illuminate the methods and strategies of case construction in trials. If the impact of evidence is understood according to the way it fits into a developing story, it becomes much easier to explain the significance of lawyers' behavior and to distinguish between the important and irrelevant aspects of cases.

In addition to its implications for legal judgment and the principles of case construction, the storytelling perspective provides a systematic way of thinking about the connections among diverse elements of trials. All too often the criminal trial is discussed as though it were an incoherent collection of variables with disembodied statistical links to verdicts and sentences. Much of the existing research on criminal trials has involved large inventories of variables such as the type of crime, the social and economic characteristics of defendants and jurors, the behavior of lawyers, the rules of the court, the deliberation procedures of juries, the group dynamics of juries, and so on. This "inventory of variables" approach to research on trials has produced an inventory of findings showing the probability with which different variables can be expected to affect the outcome of a trial. Not only are the statistical effects of the separate variables generally small, but there has been little theorizing about why different variables come into play, why they enter some cases and not others, how they operate together, and what links them systematically to the justice process. It can be shown that the characteristics of different kinds of stories can touch on virtually any feature of a trial ranging from the nature of the judge's instructions to the race of the defendant. Stories, as the mechanisms that selectively determine the relevance of various courtroom factors in any given case, provide a basis for transforming the statistical inventory of trial variables into a theoretical framework.

Perhaps the most significant application of the storytelling perspective involves clarifying the nature of bias in the justice process. Stories are symbolic reconstructions of events and actions. People who cannot manipulate symbols within a narrative format may be at a disadvantage even when, as witnesses or defendants, they are telling the truth. Moreover, the interpretation of stories requires that teller and listener share a set of norms, assumptions, and experiences. If witnesses and jurors differ in their understanding of society and social action, stories that make sense to one actor in a trial may be rejected by another. The biases that result from storytelling in trials are more subtle and more difficult to combat than the sort of bias that is based on straightforward social prejudice.

Each of the above extensions of the storytelling perspective will be developed in detail at an appropriate juncture in the argument. A model of stories as the basis for legal judgment is presented in Chapters 3 and 4. Patterns in case construction and legal strategies are analyzed in Chapters 5 and 6. Chapter 7 explores the uses of the storytelling framework to introduce theoretical coherence into the inventory of variables that has emerged from prior research. Finally, the question of bias in the justice process is addressed in Chapter 8. The remainder of this chapter is devoted to a brief introduction to the idea of stories as frameworks for legal judgment and to the way in which this idea emerged in the course of our research on criminal trials.

An Introduction to Stories and Legal Judgment

Since much of this book is devoted to precise descriptions of the uses of stories in legal judgment and trial processes, these opening remarks are intended to acquaint the reader with some very general ideas about stories. Stories are everyday communication devices that create interpretive contexts for social action. In isolation from social context, behaviors or actions are ambiguous. Much of the meaning and, therefore, the interest and importance of social activity depends on who does it, for what reasons, through what means, in what context, and with what sort of prologue and denouement. A story is simply a communicational form that provides for the development, climax, and denouement of action in the context of a defined collection of actors, means, motives, and scenes. As a result of surrounding an action with various temporal and spatial factors, a story not only focuses attention and judgment on certain key behavior (and the actors' relations to it), it also has the capacity to constrain a clear understanding about the significance of that behavior.

In everyday social situations people use stories as a means of conveying selective interpretations of social behavior to others. Stories, by starting at a particular point in time and culminating at a crucial moment or climax, also provide an understanding of an action's development. By emphasizing a particular action in a particular developmental context, stories have the capacity to create clear interpretations for social behavior—interpretations that might not have been obvious outside the story context. For example, if an individual goes on a vacation, and recounts the vacation to a friend, the account of the vacation will probably not consist of the flat documentary record of all events presented in minute descriptive detail. Rather, the account will probably emerge as a set of stories, possibly told in serial fashion following the chronology of the trip, or perhaps related in nonserial fashion and organized according to the most interesting, relevant, or similar activities. Each story will take an activity out of the historical record of the trip and provide it with an interpretive context that makes the event meaningful for both the teller and the listener, and for the relationship they share to the story subject. In this fashion, any strip of experience may be reconstructed in numerous ways, to make numerous points, relevant for different audiences.

The interpretive powers of stories take on special significance in the courtroom. The overriding judgmental tasks in a trial involve constructing an interpretation for the defendant's alleged activities and determining how that interpretation fits into the set of legal criteria that must be applied to the defendant's behavior. This judgment process is a demanding one that must take into account large amounts of information and process that information in special ways that conform to the norms of justice and the legal requirements of cases. There are several characteristics of stories that make them suitable frameworks of legal judgment.

First, stories solve the problems of information load in trials by making it possible for individuals continuously to organize and reorganize large amounts of constantly changing information. New pieces of evidence can be fit within the structural categories in an incident. Evidence gains coherence through categorical connections to story elements such as the time frames, the characters, the motives, the settings, and the means. Evidence that cannot be organized within a developing story structure can be held up immediately as a possible sign of lawyers' or witnesses' deceptions, or as an indication that the emerging story is not adequate.

Not only do stories make it possible to organize large amounts of information in coherent fashion, they are ideally suited to organizing information in the way in which it is presented in trials. Once the basic plot outline of a story begins to emerge it is possible to integrate information that is presented in the form of subplots, time disjunctures, or multiple perspectives on the same scene. Readers of novels and viewers of movies are familiar with literary devices such as flashbacks, flash-forwards, subplots, and multiple points of view. As long as a plot outline can be constructed at some point, it is possible to assimilate such disjointed information into a coherent framework. In trials cases often unfold in a more complex and disjointed fashion than do plots in novels or movies. The juror or spectator in a trial may be confronted with conflicting testimony, disorienting time lapses, the piecemeal reconstruction of a scene from the perspectives of many witnesses and experts, and a confusing array of subplots. Without the aid of an analytical device such as the story, the disjointed presentations of information in trials would be difficult, if not impossible, to assimilate.

In addition to the management of large amounts of information, legal judgment also requires the use of some analytical device that keeps the focus of attention on the alleged criminal behavior in a case and that brings the bulk of the supporting information to bear on the interpretation of that behavior. Stories set up a tension between a critical action (or series of acts) and its context. Stories not only highlight a central activity, they make it easy to sort out information according to its bearing on the interpretation of that activity. Other forms of symbolic representation may create an emphasis on scenes, moods, physical objects, or other nonbehavioral features of an incident, but stories function specifically to represent the development of some central social action. Stories are essential in trials because adjudication is dominated by the problem of interpreting disputed representations of particular social actions.

Another characteristic of legal judgments is that they must conform to specific normative standards. For example, interpretations of alleged criminal activities must take into account all the available and admissible information. Legal judgments also must be based on fair and systematic comparisons of what both sides have to say. Perhaps most important, judgments must pass the test of reasonable doubt—that is, jurors or judges must not doubt the consistency, adequacy, or plausibility of an incriminating interpretation. These normative standards of judgment seem obvious enough when viewed implicitly as things all of us are capable of doing without reflection. When examined for their formal rules or logic, however, these standards of judgment become rather formidable and mysterious.

As we show in more detail later, by looking at the structures and analytical uses of stories we can clear up the mystery of how normative standards of legal judgment are actually put in practice. Stories have implicit structures that enable people to make systematic comparisons between stories. Moreover, the structural form of a completely specified story alerts interpreters to descriptive information in a story that might be missing, and which, if filled in, could alter the significance of the action. The inadequate development of setting, character, means, or motive can, as any literature student knows, render a story's action ambiguous.[1] In a novel or film, such ambiguity may be an aesthetic flaw. In a trial, it is grounds for reasonable doubt.

A final characteristic of stories that adds to their importance in legal judgment is the fact that they produce interpretations that can be categorized easily within the legal statutes that apply to a case. Stories produce a clear definition of an action and the conditions surrounding it. This definition and its surrounding conditions can be referred directly to analogous definitions and conditions in the explanations of law contained in judges' instructions. The use of story construction and analysis skills enables complex bodies of evidence to be reduced to terms that correspond nicely to legal categories. Whether the concern is with how jurors apply legal statutes or how they process large bodies of information, stories provide the most obvious link between everyday analytical and communicational skills and the requirements of formal adjudication procedures.

The Courtroom as a Research Setting

The authoritative tone of the above discussion should not imply that we knew when we started this project that storytelling was the organizing principle of American trial justice. Nor should the reader assume that storytelling leaped to our attention the moment we entered the courtroom to begin our research. Authors, whether authors of fact or fiction, have the advantage of knowing the answers to the opening questions. Armed with this knowledge about the conclusion, they can present their subject in ways that spare the reader the pains and confusions of the discovery.

At the beginning of our investigation we were guided by much more modest and conventional orientations. We knew that some underlying judgment scheme had to exist in order for different people with vastly different relationships to the law to communicate meaningfully about the issues in legal cases. Whatever this underlying scheme was, it had to facilitate judgments that were consistent both with formal legal rules and procedures and with the commonsense understandings of most individuals who have little grasp of the law or legal processes. Not only did this mysterious judgment practice have to reconcile common sense with legal process, it also had to make it possible for average individuals to store, organize, retrieve, and process truly staggering amounts of information. Our proposed solution to the mystery of legal judgment did not materialize all at once, not did it crystallize early in our investigation.

Our theory emerged gradually over the course of more than a year of ethnographic study of criminal trials in the Superior Court of the state of Washington in King County (Seattle), Washington. Throughout our year of observation we were careful not to be distracted by "local customs" (rules and practices specific to a particular court or court system). Our attention was devoted to those things that might explain how any member of society would know how to follow the proceedings, how to participate in them, and how to "do justice" in the setting. We were alert to variations in court procedures described in the literature, and one of us had observed criminal trials in California, Michigan, and Tennessee. As our perspective emerged, it increasingly helped us to distinguish between broad characteristics of justice in the culture and artifacts of local custom.

The principal inspiration and support for our theory came from our joint or individual observation of more than sixty trials. These trials covered the entire gamut of cases eligible for trial in the Superior Court. The range was quite broad and included drunk driving, shoplifting, auto theft, forgery, narcotics violations, prostitution, rape, assault, burglary, larceny, kidnapping, and murder. Our observation of a trial normally involved much more than merely watching the proceedings. We generally arrived at the courthouse early in order to see the cast of characters assemble and prepare for the day. This proved a valuable strategy for catching bits of conversation about a case. It was useful to hear lawyers chatting among themselves, to observe discussions between lawyers and their clients and witnesses, and to hear the dialogues between jurors as they arrived at the courtroom in the morning or after lunch. We spent hours sitting in the hallways watching the parade of participants come and go. Our hallway outpost provided numerous opportunities to talk with witnesses who were scheduled to testify in a case, and to swap notes with spectators who were following a case for one reason or another. Most of these spectators had friends or relatives involved in the case. We were also attentive to the comments of the courtroom regulars—the coterie of loyal spectators who frequent the courthouse and shop among the ongoing trials much as an avid television viewer flips from one channel to the next in search of the most engrossing program. In addition, we regularly engaged various actors in quasi-interviews about a particular case or about trials in general. We found most lawyers willing to be candid in discussing their cases, the strategies they were pursuing, the special tactics they employed, and their assessments of the jury. Bailiffs and clerks provided many insights about the social dynamics of the courtroom, and about notable characteristics of cases and how they were argued. Judges were good sources of information about the behavior of lawyers, the key features of cases, and the information environment in the courtroom. In short, our network of formal and informal contacts and informants proved invaluable for validating observations, generating new ideas, and sounding out our hypotheses. We were fortunate to be able to have both structured and unstructured opportunities to discuss cases with participants. In many cases the casual observations of spectators, bailiffs, witnesses, or lawyers could be contrasted with the more detailed responses of judges or lawyers in formal interviews. This extensive feedback network made it possible to gain different perspectives about what was going on in a trial and to elicit immediate reactions to our hypotheses about what implicit practices organized judgment and communication in the courtroom. Since these implicit judgment practices were not within the immediate conscious grasp of us or our informants, we were less concerned with participants' formal descriptions of their activities than with trying to piece together the underlying logic of communication and judgment that would turn their surface descriptions of courtroom behavior into consistent and systematic explanations of legal judgment.[2]

Developing and testing our inferences also required sources of data that were more detailed and retrievable than the data we obtained through direct interviews and observation. We employed three supplementary data sources in generating and examining our hypotheses. First, we were fortunate to be granted permission to videotape an actual trial during the early stages of our research. We also obtained portions of a videotape of another trial that had been recorded as part of a legal test case to assess the impact of the electronic monitoring of trials. Since the issue of cameras in the courtroom was both legally sensitive and a natural source of fear among judges, lawyers, and clients, we are grateful for the cooperation of the entire courtroom population, which made our taping possible.[3] Second, as we began to formulate our theory of how information in trials is packaged, transmitted, and decoded within the formal structure of the trial process, we needed to simplify and test our basic concepts and variables. For these purposes we were able to run a series of simple experiments in communication with undergraduate students from the University of Washington. These experiments are discussed in Chapter 4. Finally, we needed documentary records of a large number of trials in order to determine whether our emerging ideas about the organizational formats of cases in adjudication were valid. Through the cooperation of the Washington State Court of Appeals we were able to obtain transcriptions of approximately forty cases that had been argued before the Superior Court.[4] These transcripts provide a valuable source of documentation for our analysis of the underlying features of case construction and presentation in Chapters 5 and 6.

The videotapes, communication experiments, and transcripts were used to examine our emerging hypotheses. Our first problem, however, was to generate those hypotheses. Even the most perceptive informants offered few direct insights into the nature of communication and judgment in trials. As mentioned above, participants' conscious descriptions never included references to implicit judgment practices like storytelling. When asked questions about how cases are organized and judged, or what factors affect jurors' judgments, the informants almost always referred to overt courtroom procedures such as the rules of evidence, or to simplistic behavioral explanations involving lawyers' tactics or damaging testimony. Never did informants' observations about judgment practices approach a level of sophistication that would take into account a fraction of the detail in any given trial, much less provide a general explanation of legal judgments across trials.

The tendency to produce narrow descriptions in place of general explanations was nowhere more prominent than among the lawyers and judges. As the research progressed, we quickly recognized that people did not need a formal awareness of the principles of justice and judgment to operate meaningfully in a trial. Our initial naive assumption, however, was that lawyers and judges, as seasoned observers of trials, would offer the most general insights about justice practices. To our surprise, lawyers and judges were, as a whole, unreflective about their behavior and their impact on trials. For example, in one of our first interviews we talked to a judge who had presided over a murder case in which there had been eyewitness testimony to a particularly brutal assault and murder. The jury, however, brought in an acquittal in the case. It was clear to those who sat through the trial that the defense attorney had been largely, if not solely, responsible for the miraculous verdict. We asked the judge, a veteran trial lawyer, why he thought the jury brought in an acquittal. He replied that the defense attorney was a "brilliant" lawyer. We were not satisfied that this explained anything, so we pressed our respondent on the criteria he used to identify "good lawyers." He said that this lawyer had the rare ability to "literally create doubts in the minds of jurors." In response to our questions about how these doubts were planted, he merely returned to the observation that he was a brilliant lawyer. Despite further probing and despite raising similar questions about other cases tried before this judge, we were unable to trigger any deeper observations.

Although this sort of response was by no means universal, we were struck by the frequency with which our queries to judges and lawyers elicited references to "brilliant arguments," "strong cases," "the creation of doubt," "good lawyers," and "captivated juries," with little or no understanding of just what these characterizations entailed. Even when we probed beneath the surface of such statements, we tended only to hear the collected folk wisdom of the profession, and not broad or compelling understanding of the role of lawyers in a trial. Our collection of these bits of wisdom became quite large as our research progressed. Several examples should illustrate a point that we think is important for locating a solid analytical perspective on trials.

Some lawyers feel that the "good lawyer" wins cases as a result of being able to present his or her client to the jury in the best possible light. A judge recounted that when he was a trial lawyer he used to keep an extra suit and tie in his office. If a client appeared on trial day wearing casual attire, he would be poured into the suit and taken off to court. Other lawyers claimed that the key to a trial lay in sizing up prospective jurors.

Some emphasized the importance of various rules of thumb such as rejecting mothers with daughters at home as jurors on rape cases, and screening out military personnel on delinquency and drug cases. Others stressed the importance of developing rapport with jurors during the selection of the jury panel. One lawyer even boasted that he had little concern about who sat on a jury because he felt he could win anyone over. We attended a trial of his and noted his blatant use of ingratiation routines with prospective jurors. So lengthy (and irrelevant) were these exercises that the judge eventually took over the major part of the voir dire. The lawyer attempted to use this act of the judge to win further sympathy from the jury. The jurors were apparently unmoved, as they found his client guilty.

Some of our informants recounted their courtroom secrets in the same breath with famous stories of the courtroom exploits of Clarence Darrow, Louis Nizer, Melvin Belli, or F. Lee Bailey. A bailiff in one of the courts we observed reminded one of us about the famous trial in which Darrow (we heard this story attributed to various famous lawyers) placed a wire through the length of a cigar and smoked the cigar during his opponent's closing statement. As the story goes, the jurors became so preoccupied with the ever-growing cigar ash that they missed the prosecutor's summation and acquitted the defendant. The bailiff recounted a similar story about his judge who had acquired a reputation as a brilliant deputy prosecutor when he began his law career years earlier. The story told of the only case the young prosecutor ever came close to losing. The defense had produced a key witness who began to deliver some testimony that was damaging to the prosecution case. At a critical juncture in the testimony, the prosecutor feigned reaching for a water pitcher on his table and knocked it over the edge, sending a shower of glass, water, and ice across the floor toward the witness and the jury. This action "shattered" the spell that the defense attorney was creating, and the jury, of course, found the defendant guilty.

Whether one conducts interviews with participants or reads

the voluminous literature on trials, the overwhelming impression is that trials hinge on a collection of narrow variables, such as: lines of questioning; lawyers' tactics; the testimony of key witnesses; judges' instructions; rules of evidence; the race or social status of the defendant; the nature of the crime; the class, age, sex, or racial composition of the jury; and so forth. The problem with such explanations is not so much that they are wrong, as that they are incomplete. None of the factors mentioned above is likely to be a determining force in more than a small percentage of cases. Thus, they offer no general explanation about what it is that organizes communication and judgment in trials in general. Moreover, since isolated variables like the race of the defendant, or the wording of the judge's instructions, or the dispositions of jurors toward authority, explain only a small percentage of the variance in trial outcomes, the important question about such variables is when they operate and what brings them into play. Understanding the implicit judgment practices used by participants in trials would make it possible to explain when factors like defendant's race or lawyer's tactics become relevant in making a judgment about a case, and when they have no place in making a practical judgment.

As mentioned earlier, participants in trials have no practical need to understand the implicit judgment practices in the systematic organizing principles underlying trials. Lawyers, judges, witnesses, and jurors will behave effectively in terms of these principles whether or not they understand them at a conscious level. These two facts were easier to grasp intellectually than to fit into our methodological framework. However, after dozens of interviews produced little more than superficial descriptions of trials, we simply asked informants to describe what they thought particular cases were about. A second shift in our research approach involved the way in which we listened to our informants' responses. Instead of concentrating on their specific statements and formal explanations, we began listening for common ways in which cases were summarized, evaluated, and described.

After we turned our attention to the way in which people organized information about cases for descriptive purposes, a striking pattern began to emerge. Virtually all members of the courtroom scene, from judges to spectators, framed the key judgmental issues in trials by organizing the opposing cases into stories about the alleged criminal behavior. At first, stories seemed like such familiar and obvious descriptive devices that we did not pay much attention to them. However, the more we listened to the ways in which people used stories to discuss cases, the more we realized that stories were not just descriptive devices. It became clear that stories served powerful analytic functions. The analytic uses of stories made them prime candidates for the everyday judgment practices that enable diverse individuals to communicate sensibly and perform their roles properly within the formal legal process of the trial.

Chapter 2
Formal Legal Procedures and Implicit Judgment Practices

In Chapter 1 we discussed the importance of stories as means of organizing information in a judicial process. We suggested that stories enable people, particularly jurors, to keep track of the information presented in a trial, to interpret the central issues in cases by identifying them as central actions in stories, and to make normative judgments about these interpretations. In this chapter we address the role that judicial procedures play in justice processes. If stories are to be recognized as integral features of trials, the relationship between stories and formal justice procedures must be clarified.

Any method of settling disputes has both procedural and substantive features. The procedural features are the rituals that are followed for presenting the dispute to a judging body. The substantive features are the facts that are considered relevant to the dispute. Both procedural and substantive aspects vary from one society to another. The configuration of these features reflects what is considered necessary for doing justice in a society. In other words, both the form and the content of the judicial process must be consistent with what members of a society need to assess a situation and to determine a fair and just settlement.

What rituals are followed and what information is presented in this process depend on what is best suited to the cultural bases for judgment. For example, in societies that rely on supernatural beings to issue judgments, procedures will be very different from those in societies that rely solely on human judges. Judgment processes also vary from one culture to another according to the importance attributed to circumstances and contexts as modifiers of the meaning of actions. Judgment processes in societies in which the meanings of social behavior are narrowly constrained by norms will require less information than in societies in which the meanings of behavior are broad or ambiguous.

In this chapter we will see how the procedures adopted for settling disputes in various societies allow the participants to present the substantive material needed for interpreting and judging a dispute. This discussion illustrates three points about justice processes and the role of implicit judgment operations (e.g., storytelling) in them. First, the procedures for doing justice vary both within and across societies, and these procedures can change with time and social conditions. Second, even though justice procedures may vary, they have the common function of enabling members of society to understand (and in some cases apply) the grounds for fair and just settlements of disputes. This implies that if the terms of justice are to make sense to the average members of a society, the formal procedures of justice must somehow incorporate everyday means of communication and judgment like storytelling. Third, through examining the relationship between the formal procedures and the everyday judgment practices involved in doing justice, it is possible to expose the meanings of objectivity and fairness in a society. The presentation of information in disputes in ways that are regarded as objective and impartial provides a peephole on the society's perception of reality. As a result of this perspective it is possible to explore the functions of justice in society.

Varieties of Adjudication Procedures

It is easy to think of our ways of doing justice through adjudication as uniquely just and unchanging. In fact, the idea of justice seems synonymous with permanent procedures and unchanging principles. It is important to recognize, however, that justice procedures vary across societies as social circumstances and belief systems vary. Therefore, any society's justice procedures will seem sensible and enduring to its members in comparison to the methods in other cultures. It is, after all, through exposure to adjudication that members of society come in contact with the broadest representations of the binding moral community to which they belong. Adjudication processes confront active participants and distant spectators with the demands of a society and the consequences of ignoring them.

Despite the appearance that justice procedures are unchanging, they do, in fact, change along with changes in social organization and belief. Thus, justice processes not only vary across societies, they also change within a society as functions of time and circumstance. Our point in illustrating these variations within and between societies is to show the importance of everyday knowledge and knowledge structures like stories in the production of justice. The fact that justice processes change and differ and involve commonsense understandings does not, however, imply that justice is a meaningless or empty concept. In fact, for justice to have meaning, it *must* reflect the social understandings common in a society and it must incorporate changes in those understandings over time.

One example of how justice procedures change in conjunction with social change is provided by the evolution of the idea of a jury of peers. Initially the jury in the English common law tradition was composed of people who knew the defendant. The definition of a peer implied someone who knew well the context in which the defendant lived and could understand the circumstances that surrounded the defendant's actions. Such knowledge was considered crucial to arriving at a fair verdict. Current practice is nearly the reverse. Jurors not only must not know the defendant personally, they must not have any preconceived notions about the defendant's character or propensity to have committed a crime. It is now considered contrary to the justice process for a member of the jury to have any direct knowledge of the defendant's life circumstances other than those presented in the trial. Even this definition of a jury of peers may be changing as evidenced by increasing demands for representation of the defendant's demographic characteristics in jury pools. This demographic definition of peers differs in subtle ways from both of the past legal uses cited above. Such changes in formal procedures and principles indicate corresponding changes in the ways in which adjudicators actually organize and judge the evidence in cases.

The relationships between formal justice procedures and the implicit practices through which members of society actually do justice are illustrated even more clearly by the varieties of adjudication practices in different societies. Cross-cultural variations in adjudication also indicate that the idea of storytelling in American trials is not as strange as it may appear initially. There are various forms of adjudication, and each form involves different implicit judgment practices and displays a different notion of how to do justice. One form is oath taking; another is trial by ordeal; another is trial by jury or judge. There are undoubtedly other forms. These three examples, however, will serve to illustrate that the achievement of justice is not so much dependent on the procedure, per se, as on the societal acceptance of the procedure and the coherence of societal beliefs with the procedure.

In societies that handle the adjudication of disputes primarily through the administration of oaths, the charges and denials of the disputants are presented in some public forum with the community in attendance. The parties involved are led through the oath (or assisted with relevant paraphernalia) by some community justice official, chief, or religious leader. The setting, the rites, and the cast of characters may contribute to the legitimacy and regularity of the proceedings, but the pronouncement itself establishes a framework for thinking about the transgression and a method for resolving it. Oaths generally call upon gods or divine spirits to witness testimony and to assist in judgment.

A Bedouin oath is fairly typical. As Roberts describes it (from a study by Musil), the procedure begins when a judge steps before the disputants and the assembled community. With a saber he draws a circle whose diameter is intersected by five vertical lines. The witness then steps inside the circle and, facing south, begins his testimony with the affirmation, "A false oath is the ruin of the descendants, for he who swears falsely is insatiable in his desire of gain and does not fear his Lord." [1]

In Bedouin adjudication, as with any justice process, the procedures for bringing together the disputants, presenting charges, and administering the oath must be distinguished from the implicit understandings that make the oaths significant, and that enable the judge and the community to grasp the signs that reveal the judgment in a case. In some cases, the determination of judgment is a simple matter because the accused or the witness refuses to take the oath, and refusal to take the oath is clear proof of guilt or false accusation. If, however, all parties take their oaths, legal judgment and the satisfactory resolution of the dispute depend on broad religious understandings and universal faith in divine intervention.

Taking an oath generally places one, and often one's ancestors, descendants, and community at the mercy of a deity. Moreover, the delivery of an oath assures the community and the disputants that the evidence pertinent to the case has been put in a form suitable for transmission to a supreme being who acts as the ultimate judge. Any oath behavior that does not call for an obvious remedy from the community will be reviewed by a god who will determine the absolute truth of the matter and impose a just resolution. The community generally rests assured that the deity can choose any number of ways of dealing with false witnesses. A punishment may be visited upon a perjurer in another life. Shame or misfortune may be brought upon the person's entire lineage. In some instances, the supreme being may even bestow immediate physical punishment on the offender to provide an example for the whole community. The signs of god's judgment in the here and now may include such catastrophes as madness, sickness, accident, or untimely death.

In contrast to adjudication processes centered around oaths, there are a great number of processes that impose some test or ordeal on the disputants. In societies that rely on these processes, disputes are generally regarded by community adjudicators as striking at the material or spiritual well-being of the entire community. The tests (usually ordeals of various sorts) provide speedy and generally conclusive proof or refutation of claims, thereby relieving public doubts or anxieties (often at considerable cost to the disputants).

Ordeals all share the characteristic capacity to produce some involuntary physical response in the witness. These responses may include burning, blistering, bleeding, vomiting, flinching, floating, fainting, drowning (possibly followed by floating or sinking), failure of strength, or collapse from physical exhaustion. The appearance of such a response during or following an ordeal is generally taken as a sign of guilt. Occasionally the community adjudicators are given some margin of flexibility in interpretation, as in cases of burning or blistering in which the intensity of the response may be taken into account in rendering judgment or prescribing remedy.

Ordeals involving scalding or boiling are probably the most common. For example, Barton reported a procedure among the Ifugao in which guilt or innocence depended on whether the accused flinched while extracting a pebble from a pot of boiling water.[2] Linton reported another scalding ordeal used by the Tanala:

Water was boiled in a large pot and a stone fastened to a cord, like a plumb-line. The stone was dropped vertically into the pot, but was not submerged. The cord was attached to a stick which rested across the mouth of the pot so that the stone hung about 5 mm. above the water. The suspect's hand was washed and examined to see whether he had any scars on it, also whether it had been rubbed with medicine. After the Anakandriana had made the usual invocation, the accused approached the pot and seized the stone from below, plunging his hand into the boiling water. He then plunged his hand into cold water. The hand was bandaged and the accused shut up in a guarded house. The next morning all assembled to see his condition. If there were blisters on the hand he was guilty. If accused of sorcery he was killed on the spot, or, if the king was merciful, he was expelled and all his goods seized.[3]

This Tanala ordeal again illustrates the pattern of a set of formal procedures (preparation of water, arrangement of stone, invocation by the ritual leader, etc.) that elicits an underlying judgment routine (the cosmology by which the ordeal's results become meaningful). The underlying judgment practice permits the community to determine the status of the charges, evaluate the response of the accused, and make judgments about the outcome. This underlying practice also constitutes a test for the evidence that fits the episode into the broadly shared understandings about supernatural and mundane realities in which justice is embedded.

Trials by judge or jury rely wholly upon human judgment for verdict and sanction. In one form or another, the stories of the various actors are presented to a judging body. In most trials at least the defendant and the complainant present their respective versions of the dispute. Witnesses may be used to corroborate accounts or to give evidence about the character of the defendant or the complainant. Questions are usually asked either by the judging body or by some adjunct of the court. The outcome often takes the form of a verdict that is returned after some deliberation among judges or members of a jury. Sanctions may either be automatically applied as a consequence of the verdict, or be tailored to resolving the specific dispute. In some societies, such as the Zapotec, the outcome is not necessarily a pronouncement of innocence or guilt but often takes the form of advice from the judge to the disputing parties about a way to resolve the dispute.[4]

Whatever the formal adjudication procedure, it must be perceived as capable of producing a fair settlement. Formal procedures must present disputed facts in ways that make it possible for members to use implicit judgment practices to judge those facts. The examination of justice processes in different societies demonstrates the existence of a variety of implicit judgment practices involved in the production of justice. Perhaps more important, as shown in the next section, these implicit practices (like storytelling) actually determine the outcomes of justice.

Adjudication as Formal Legal Procedure and Implicit Judgment Practice

Justice processes that rely on stories or other forms of discourse may differ in terms of the kinds of principles that underlie the uses and interpretation of the discourse. All discourse-based methods of judgment, however, share one important characteristic: they provide organizing structures for using common-sense understandings about such bases of legal judgment as right and wrong, fact and fiction, and social harmony. The idea that commonsense understandings are somehow introduced into most justice processes is, of course, nothing new. For example, Vinogradoff long ago noticed the connection between common sense and legal judgment in justice processes that entail the determination of fact and the legal status of action.

Has a murder been committed or not? or is it a case of manslaughter? or of a brawl which led to the infliction of a fatal wound? has this particular man, the prisoner, committed the crime? did he do it of his own notion or at the instigation of another? In so far the examination turns on matters of ordinary social experience, and therefore the decision of all such questions is commonly left to a jury composed of laymen.[5]

The questions that remain unanswered are: (1) how the collection of commonsense understandings about cause and effect, likelihood, propriety, logic, and social aesthetics are screened, selected, and applied to specific accounts, and (2) what role courtroom procedures play in this process. By examining the judgment routines in different societies it may be possible to begin to answer these questions.

Consider the relation between formal adjudication procedures and implicit judgment practices found in Messenger's

study of Anang trials.[6] In many respects, the formal legal procedures used by the Anang are similar to those in most societies
that rely on human judgment for resolving disputes. There are
formal rules for convening the court, introducing evidence, taking oaths, hearing charges, eliciting testimony, and judging the
issues in cases. In addition to these straightforward aspects of
legal process, however, every trial contains a curious practice
that seems to fall in a category apart from the formal rules of the
trial. At key junctures in every trial the participants (plaintiff,
defendants, witnesses, oath givers, judges) represented the issues in the case, as they understood them, in the form of cryptic
proverbs. For example, in one trial the plaintiff presented his
evidence against the man he accused of robbing him and closed
the case against him with the saying, "If a dog plucks palm
fruits from a cluster, he does not fear a porcupine." In response
to this proverb, the defendant contended that the plaintiff did
not have any evidence against him and was trying to bias the
case by introducing (through the proverb) the inadmissible fact
that the defendant had been found guilty of robbery in the past.
The defendant summarized this argument and secured his acquittal by invoking the proverb, "A single partridge flying
through the bush leaves no path."

Lay participants in Anang trials were not the only users of
proverbs. Court officials also invoked proverbs as a means of
framing key judgmental issues. For example, a court officer who
administered oaths to witnesses could not induce the plaintiff in
an assault case to swear an oath prior to delivering his charge
against the defendant. The oath giver provided the court with
an interpretation of the plaintiff's behavior with the proverb, "If
an animal resembles a palm fruit cluster, how can it be butch-
ered?" In ruling against the plaintiff in this case, the judge
noted the propriety of the proverb, and explained his decision
in the case with a proverbial admonition to the plaintiff, "If you
visit the home of the toads, stoop."

Although the Anang do not consider the proverbs to have any
systematic function in the justice process, there is evidence

to indicate that the proverbs play a central role in making the issues in a case open to judgment. The patterns of usage reported by Messenger indicate that proverbs are ways of placing the central issues in Anang disputes in critical contexts. These contexts enable participants in trials to juxtapose the facts in a case with various social norms that might be appropriate for judging the case. Some proverbs provide a better fit for the issues and evidence than others, and the degree of fit of a particular proverb enables participants to determine both the social principles applicable to the case, and the certainty or "objectivity" with which those principles can be shown to encompass all the relevant concerns in the dispute. These uses of proverbs in arriving at objective and confident legal judgments in Anang can be illustrated with one of the examples introduced earlier.

One of the proverbs used in the robbery case mentioned above was, "If a dog plucks palm fruits from a cluster, he does not fear a porcupine." Messenger determined that this saying referred to the cluster of fruit on the palm oil tree which is protected by sharp needles that inflict pain on those who are bold enough to pick the fruit. However, once the fruit is tasted the pain may be worth enduring in the future, and the offender's fear of other forbidden fruit and its protective warnings may be diminished. This proverb was used by the plaintiff to set up the inference that since the defendant had committed robbery in the past, he would be likely to do so again under the circumstances described by the plaintiff. This linkage between a conventional social understanding and the specific facts in the case might have carried the day had the defendant not produced a proverb that invoked a more powerful norm and, at the same time, provided an even more tightly constrained interpretation for the evidence. The defendant noted that the plaintiff had not proved that he was present at the scene of the crime; therefore, the defendant argued, the case against him was based only on the fact that he had been found guilty of robbery in the past, and this past crime prejudiced the community against him. He represented his isolation from the community with the proverb, "A single partridge flying through the bush leaves no path." This proverb reminded the judge that social isolation makes it easy to condemn an individual, but that it would be unjust to do so. The judge accepted the defendant's proverbial interpretation of the case over the one offered by the plaintiff.

As this example indicates, proverbs are the means through which participants in Anang trials organize the information in a case, compare the strength or "goodness of fit" of different ways of organizing and interpreting the information, and derive the normative implications associated with different ways of interpreting the information. In the robbery case, two possible proverbial interpretations were offered, each providing some grounds for interpreting some of the facts in the case. One interpretation, however, constrained more of the facts within a more compelling social norm, thereby providing a stronger basis for judgment.

Objective legal judgment in Anang does not exist in some metaphysical world apart from the actual legal procedures employed in Anang courts. Objective legal judgment is defined by the search for the proverb that best captures the issues and evidence in a case. Since proverbs are, by definition, the most universally accepted statements of normative propositions among the Anang, the proverb that provides the best fit for a case also introduces an established and enduring principle of judgment appropriate for the legal resolution of the case. In this sense, objective judgment for the Anang is based on standard procedures that are agreed upon by all, and that introduce external social norms as bases for judging specific disputes in ways that can be held up for public inspection. These aspects of Anang judgment practices transform "objective" legal judgments from vague metaphysical concepts into observable phenomena based upon documentable social practices.

Gluckman's study of the Barotse is another ethnography that shows how formal justice procedures accommodate commonsense understandings in the justice process via the use of everyday forms of discourse.[7] Gluckman's descriptions of Barotse adjudication demonstrate convincingly that the forms of discourse in judge or jury systems must constrain the practical application of commonsense understanding to specific cases in ways that are consistent with legal principles.

The narratives provided by disputants in Barotse courts are constructed to demonstrate to judges that the behavior mentioned in the charges is either consistent or inconsistent with the set of norms and probabilities that conform to the Barotse commonsense criteria of *mutu yanaga*, which, according to Gluckman, corresponds to the Western jurisprudential standard of the "reasonable man."[8] Whenever the narrative structure in Barotse trials wanders from easily grasped claims about the circumstances that make key behaviors "reasonable," Barotse judges either call for a reformulation of the narrative or impose a normative standard (judgment) on the account that makes better sense of the described circumstances: "The kuta's [the court's] main technique in cross examination is therefore to state the norms of behavior of a specific position, as the reasonable man would react in a perhaps unique situation. Whenever a party's own account shows deviations from these norms, the judges are able to attack him."[9]

In this fashion, commonsense standards of judgment and the narrative structure used to present a case operated in a dialectical tension, with the narrative structure invoking particular norms, and with more comprehensive competing norms being offered to subsume inadequate narratives. This interplay among narrative structure, commonsense understandings, and legal principles is illustrated nicely by a case described by Gluckman in which a villager charged an *induna* (a village chieftain) with attacking him and contributing to his defeat and humiliation in a personal fight between him and the *induna's* son. The villager told his story first. He said that the *induna's* son had made advances toward his wife. They started to fight over this question of honor at the villager's home, but his wife's father ordered the fighting stopped. The villager followed the *induna's* son home after the fight. When he entered the *induna's* courtyard he was attacked by the son and some siblings. At this point the *induna* appeared, but rather than stopping the fight (as the villager's father-in-law had done), he joined the fracas. He grabbed the villager by the wrist while his children attacked him. The villager screamed that the *induna* was "breaking him." The villager's wife arrived at this point and asked the *induna* to stop the fight. The *induna* dropped his hold on the villager, but he went to get his whip and, later, a stamping pole. Although he did not use these weapons, neither did he stop the fight, which ended with the villager's defeat.

The *induna* then gave his version of the incident. His account began by providing another explanation for the fight. He said the villager had insulted his son. The *induna* went to the villager's home to try to stop the impending fight, but the two men had already gone. When he returned home he found the villager fighting with his children. He grabbed the villager by the wrist to pull him out of the fight. He got the whip to scare all of the fighters, and he got the stamping pole to make sure that nobody involved would use it. He concluded by saying that such incidents wouldn't happen in the first place if the villager's wife (and her sisters) did not act like whores.

The judgment of the case involved two points established through comparing the accounts. First, reasoned the judges, if the *induna* was trying to stop the fight, why did he seize the man who was on the ground rather than the children who were on top of him? Second, if, in fact, the *induna* seized the man's wrist in order to help him, why did he release his wrist when the man's wife asked the *induna* to "stop fighting"? These seemed to be deviations from the way a normal person stopping a fight would act. Moreover, the use of a whip to break up a fight would have been an action unworthy of an *induna*. Thus the *induna*'s account was an inadequate response to the villager's account according to both empirical and normative standards of reasonableness. As a result, the judges concluded that the villager's story was correct and that the *induna* was guilty of fighting.

Once it is clear that implicit judgment practices (and not the formal procedures of a justice process) are responsible for the production of justice, it is possible to explore the meanings of justice in society. If the analysis of justice processes concentrates only on formal procedures, it is difficult to say much beyond the obvious observation that justice is what justice does (or, a justice process is a justice process is a justice process). If, however, adjudication is seen to be based on the selective application of social understandings, then the ways in which these beliefs and values are applied to cases explain what justice means to people and what values the justice process represents. In the next section, the implicit judgment practice of storytelling is examined for its implications about the nature of justice in American society.

Storytelling and the Social Functions
of American Trial Justice

It appears initially that the principles of justice introduced into formal adjudication processes such as trials are obvious. Everyone knows that adjudication procedures are designed to guarantee due process, to promote fair and impartial judgments, and to decide questions of fact in uniform and objective ways. Above all, the procedures in criminal trials seem designed to promote objectivity in the process of making judgments about carefully circumscribed issues.

"Objectivity," however, as most citizens and scholars use it to describe principles of justice in America, is not a very revealing term. Referring to justice processes as objective does not imply that they hold any special purchase on revealed truth or infallibility. The judgments made in criminal trials can be regarded as objective only in the sense that they reflect the use of a uniform and agreed-upon set of legal procedures and judgment practices. In other words, the principle of objectivity is embodied in the standardized set of formal procedures and implicit judgment practices in trials, and not in any metaphysical criteria of truth or fact. If the meaning of legal objectivity (and related concepts of uniformity, fact finding, fairness, etc.) is involved with the practices for producing legal judgments, then the nature of these practices provides the only concrete meaning for the concept. In other words, the concept of objectivity is largely a procedural notion based on the uniform structural and interpretive characteristics of stories that enable diverse individuals to hear cases in fairly uniform ways. However, the ways in which stories represent the incidents in legal disputes produce often radical transformations of "reality" that are hard to reconcile with commonsense understandings about objectivity.

Judgments based on story construction are, in many important respects, unverifiable in terms of the reality of the situation that the story represents. Adjudicators judge the plausibility of a story according to certain structural relations among symbols in the story. Although documentary evidence may exist to support most symbolizations in a story, both the teller and the interpreter of a story *always* have some margin of control over the definition of certain key symbols. Therefore, stories are judged in terms of a combination of the documentary or "empirical" warrants for symbols and the internal structural relations among the collection of symbols presented in the story. In other words, we judge stories according to a dual standard of "did it happen that way?" and "could it have happened that way?" In no case can "empirical" standards alone produce a completely adequate judgment, and, as we show in later chapters, there are cases in which the structural characteristics are far and away the critical elements in determining the truth of a story.

This means that, within certain limits, disputants have some escape from (i.e., cannot be held accountable for) the reality of their dispute. This margin of escape is widest when questions of "circumstances" are at stake. Not only are cases based on "circumstantial" evidence the most difficult ones to prove, but one may be able to plead a defensible case based on the claim that one was a "victim of circumstances." In other words, the implicit judgment practices used in formal adjudications not only give disputants some freedom to reinterpret what happened to them (or what they did), but if they can characterize plausibly the incident in terms of circumstances beyond their control, there may well be legal standards or normative dispositions to absolve them of guilt.

It is in many ways a curious and salient cultural tendency to think of "circumstances" as causal or dynamic forces in behavior. This is a special way of thinking about reality. It is based on the premise that reality itself can be misleading, illusory, or unjust. This perspective on reality also implies that we understand that symbolization, communication, and interpretation are prime moving forces in social life. Though we may not recognize this perspective explicitly, it is evident in the processes we rely on to make our reality meaningful. Although these "creative" processes construct the reality in which we live, they are also fallible, subject to misuse and capable of presenting false images to participants in situations. In short, we recognize that we can become victims of our own symbols and our own communication processes.

If there is any doubt that questions of fate, circumstances, and reality are central to the scope of justice in this society, consider the overwhelming importance of these themes in various forms of our popular culture: detective and mystery novels, human interest stories, movies, dramas, news stories, soap operas, and even situation comedies. Many of us have, for example, suffered with the protagonists of Alfred Hitchcock films like *Strangers on a Train*, *The Man Who Knew Too Much*, *The Wrong Man*, *North by Northwest*, and *Vertigo*. In these and other films, Hitchcock takes an ordinary person and envelops him or her in a web of circumstance and intrigue beyond comprehension. The victim becomes estranged from the real world; doubted by friends; hunted, trapped, or ignored by the law enforcement agencies that would ordinarily have been petitioned for help. The world, in short, becomes blind to the circumstances of the hapless victim, and efforts to correct misunderstandings or locate the forces responsible for the situation only make matters worse. We, the audience, see the situation as it really is, but understand with the victim that every move, every statement, every effort to control the situation will only take on meaning in the context of events and circumstances beyond his or her control.

In another vein, we have watched or read courtroom melodramas (Perry Mason stories are the prototype) in which the great lawyer agrees to take a hopeless case and build a defense against all odds. The evidence against the client is so damaging that even the lawyer suffers doubts about his faith in the client's earnest claims of innocence. We suffer through the maze of dead ends before the trial. The prosecution case is ironclad. The trial only makes things worse. Each witness contributes to the inescapable conclusion that the defendant must have committed the crime. Then something occurs to the lawyer—perhaps as a result of something a witness said, or a remark the client made, or a change of heart on the part of a conspiratorial witness, or a stroke of genius on the lawyer's part. A new interpretation for the facts begins to emerge. Indeed, a new "story" takes shape. A key witness is recalled. The new version of the crime is unfolded through a brilliant line of questioning. The witness is trapped. The web of circumstances is unraveled. Justice is done. Reality and justice become reconciled.

The variations on these themes are endless. There are the classic detective novels about "guilty" clients who have been framed, and about suspects in murders who are freed from suspicion only through the detective's careful disassembling of a chain of circumstance. There are situation comedies based on cases of mistaken identity, accidental involvement in unfamiliar situations, and benign activities that trap the protagonist in an increasingly inescapable charade. There are human interest stories about persons who become the hapless victims of impersonal bureaucracies. In short, our everyday encounters with popular culture are filled with "lessons" about how reality is constructed, how fragile or transparent reality can be, how we can become victimized by circumstances beyond our control or beyond the naive expectations we had when we entered a situation, and how we can attempt to cope with these situations (and represent ourselves to agents of justice) should they occur.

These primitive understandings about reality and the relationship between reality and justice account both for the salience of these recurring themes in forms of popular culture and for the ways in which audiences become involved with them. Why are we so prone to identify with victims of circumstance and agonize with their plight? Why does this theme never seem to exhaust possible plots and expressions? How is it that even though we "know" that the defendant in the courtroom melodrama and the suspect in the murder mystery will be proved innocent, we can be engrossed by the story and surprised and relieved by its ending? We cannot hope to answer such complex questions here, but we can offer a few thoughts on the subject. We identify with victims of circumstances because we recognize the role of circumstance, and the fate of its victims, in daily life. We understand that the battle against an uncomprehending world and a perverse reality is among the most terrifying and hopeless fights a person can wage. (So profound is this concern in our society that ego defenses involving the control of fate are among the core elements in many psychological syndromes.) We can become absorbed in such familiar scenarios because they all contain a tension, indeed a troubling contradiction, between how things ought to work out in life (justice) and how things, in practice, can work out differently (circumstance). It is the search for a resolution between justice and circumstance that makes new variations on these old themes worth our attention. We can be surprised by the inevitable happy ending because we have not anticipated the particular reconstruction of events that yields the resolution of the contradiction. Inherent in our concern about control over reality is the understanding that configurations of events, actions, and information can seem compelling and substantial, yet a slight shift in perspective, the addition of a bit of new information, can reveal, suddenly, a new image.

Such experiences with popular culture draw upon deep understandings about our world. In this light it is, perhaps, not so surprising that we would weight our justice processes in favor of a margin of escape from circumstances—circumstances that lead to behavior that is misconstrued, to imputed motives that are not intended, or to accusations that are false but well-meaning. Stories are important in this context because they are capsule versions of reality. They pick up an incident and set it down in another social context. In this transition, the data can be selected, the historical frame can be specified, the situational factors can be redefined, and "missing observations" can be implied. In short, a situation can be re-presented in a form consistent with an actor's perspective and interests both during and after the incident. The use of stories in adjudication allows people some margin of freedom to re-present a historical reality in a form that might free them from victimization by circumstance.

If, in American adjudication, it is the story that creates the basis of judgment, the ways in which stories affect the structure and interpretation of information must be explained. The next chapter presents a simple explanation of how stories constrain the interpretation of facts in legal cases.

PART II
A THEORY OF STORY
CONSTRUCTION AND SOCIAL
JUDGMENT

Chapter 3
Stories and the Construction
of Legal Judgments

Stories organize information in ways that help the listener to perform three interpretive operations.[1] First, the interpreter must be able to locate the central action in a story. This is the key behavior around which the point of the story is drawn. Second, the interpreter must construct inferences about the relationships among the surrounding elements in the story that impinge on the central action. The connections among this cast of supportive symbols create the interpretive context for the action or behavior at the center of the story. Finally, the network of symbolic connections drawn around the central action in a story must be tested for internal consistency and descriptive adequacy or completeness. This simply means that the interpreter must determine that the various inferences that make up a general interpretation for a story are both mutually compatible (in light of what is known about similar episodes in the real world) and sufficiently specified to yield an unequivocal interpretation. These three cognitive operations constitute the explanation of legal judgment developed in this chapter. Before we describe how stories are geared structurally to these operations, it may be useful to work through a hypothetical example of how these operations enter into the judgments of average persons serving as jurors.

Suppose that you have been selected to serve as a juror on a murder trial. The state opens its case by announcing that a woman has been killed. The police found her body in bed. They had been called that morning by her husband who, according to his story, became alarmed when his efforts to awaken his sleeping wife had failed. The coroner's autopsy determined that the cause of death was poisoning. The poison had been administered the evening before. There was no evidence of any third party in the home that evening, nor was there any known motive that would account for the involvement of an outside party in the incident. There was, however, a motive for the husband. He had been named as the beneficiary in a large insurance policy taken out shortly before the woman's death. The prosecutor concludes his statement by telling you that the state will prove that the defendant killed his wife in order to receive the insurance money. Even though the central action in the incident has not been specified as yet, we know already how to recognize it. We know that the central action will be some behavior that could have caused the death (e.g., the wife might have taken an overdose of sleeping pills or the husband might have poisoned her bedtime cocoa). It is this behavior that must be interpreted in order to determine whether the death was suicide, accident, or homicide. Somehow from the sketchy story presented in the opening remarks of the prosecutor we have developed criteria for separating the central action out of all the other actions described in the forthcoming testimony. This is the first cognitive operation facilitated by stories.

The state then produces three witnesses who offer accounts that fit into the general story told by the prosecutor. First, the detective assigned to the case testifies that he questioned a man at the scene of the death who identified himself as the husband of the deceased. The man said he had been the only person with the woman during the past twenty-four hours. That man is in the courtroom today. He is the defendant. The detective goes on to say that when he asked the man about the existence of any insurance policies on the deceased, the man became visibly nervous. The defense lawyer objects to this speculation about his client's nervousness, and the judge orders it stricken from the record. The next prosecution witness is the coroner. He testifies that he performed an autopsy and determined the cause of death to be a massive dose of strychnine. Finally, an insurance agent takes the stand and describes an incident that occurred a week prior to the death. The defendant came to his office and made arrangements to purchase a large policy on his wife. The woman did not accompany her husband to the office. The man took the policy with him and returned several days later with her signature. The policy named the defendant as beneficiary.

At this point the state rests its case. Suppose that the defense does not put on a case, but simply argues that the state has failed to prove that the defendant had anything to do with the woman's death. The defense lawyer tells you that the prosecution case is based on the flimsiest of circumstantial evidence. He also tells you that the prosecutor has not even shown how the woman was killed, let alone whether the defendant was involved in any way. What would you do?

It is true that the central action has not been defined formally, but you probably have made some connections among isolated elements that surround the as yet unspecified central action in the prosecutor's story. For example, from all possible categorizations that could be made to establish relationships between the two actors in the story, you have probably selected "marriage" and "insurance." You connect the actors in the story with categories like "husband-wife" and "beneficiary-insured." The connection "husband-wife" gives us access to general empirical knowledge about that sort of relationship. We may use that knowledge to establish other connections. For example, we may see significance in the connection between the fact that the actors are husband and wife and the fact that they were at home alone on the evening in question. We might even infer from these connections that the sort of intimacy characterized by this relationship could have provided many opportunities for such a crime to be committed while they were alone in each other's presence. The connection between "insured" and "beneficiary" might take us along another generalized path to the act in question. For example, we know that beneficiaries collect money from policies upon the death of the insured. The policy in this case was large. The beneficiary would stand to gain great wealth from the woman's death. The beneficiary was the husband. Perhaps he had a motive. The connections shown in Figure 1 may now exist in our minds. These inferences represent the second type of cognitive operation facilitated by story structure.

The inferences established thus far among the elements surrounding the central action in the story do have a certain appeal. However, the defense response to this case is credible also. None of the actions contained in the prosecution story really qualifies as a good central action. We simply do not have a description of an action committed by the husband that could be called "murderous" in the context of the inferences already established. We know that there are still too many gaps in the story to establish a tight causal sequence leading necessarily to a murderous act. How do we know that the inferences drawn thus far, while internally consistent, are incomplete from the standpoint of establishing a clear interpretation for the incident? We can know these things only if the story structure is parallel to some general cognitive model of the systematic relations

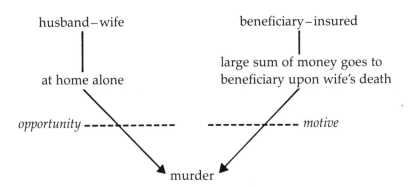

Figure 1. Partial Inferences about a Murder Case Based on the First Two Cognitive Operations of the Storytelling Model

among analogous elements in real-world situations. The third type of cognitive operation associated with stories allows us to know whether the inferences drawn from a story are consistent with other familiar situations. It also helps us determine if the inferences are complete or systematic enough to yield a clear interpretation for the story. Finally, if the story is judged incomplete, this cognitive operation provides us with knowledge about what is missing.

In this case, it is obvious what is missing. Either we need information about the action that directly induced the poison into the victim's body, or we need to establish a sequence of actions that would leave no doubt about the description of that action. Imagine that the prosecution had called another witness. This person, a neighbor of the defendant, testifies that he was watching television the night of the death. He went to the kitchen during a commercial and as he passed a window noticed a light in the garage next door. Thinking that something might be amiss, he went to the window that provided a better view of the garage. He saw the defendant emerge from the garage carrying a box of rat poison. The defendant then went into the house. The prosecutor now recalls the detective to the stand. The detective testifies that the police crime lab analyzed a sample of ashes from the fireplace of the house and found abnormal amounts of strychnine along with other elements commonly found in rat poison. The coroner then resumes the stand to testify that the woman ingested some hot chocolate shortly before retiring. Such a drink would disguise the flavor of the poison.

These additional elements would allow most of us to infer that the husband poisoned the wife's bedtime drink and then destroyed the evidence in the fireplace. These connections between the husband and the probable means of death tighten our inference that the death was probably not attributable to accident, suicide, or some outside party. It also strengthens the conclusion that the husband was responsible for the act that killed his wife, and the circumstances indicate that he probably intended to kill her. We now have a more adequate explanation for the incident—an explanation that offers a clear interpretation for the central action in question in the trial. This explanation was formed by working back and forth between isolated connections among story symbols and the way these symbols fit into our generalized notions of social life.

Although the interpretation diagrammed in Figure 2 may not satisfy everyone "beyond a reasonable doubt," it will come much closer to doing so than the first version of the story. The point that emerges from this exercise is that we know implicitly how to connect relevant symbols in a story and how to systematize and interpret their bearing on the action that lies at the center of the story. We can, then, compare this interpretation with our understanding of social reality. Through this procedure we

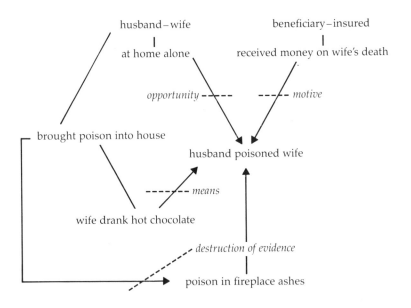

Figure 2. Completed Inferences about a Murder Case Based on the Storytelling Model

distinguish the central action in the story from other, peripheral actions, and we either assign a clear interpretation to it or determine that the information presented in the story is not sufficient to warrant a confident judgment. With this example in place, we turn now to a formal description of the three types of cognitive operations in a story model of legal judgment.

Identifying the Central Action

The first cognitive operation elicited by stories is the isolation of some central action around which the story develops. The most obvious characteristics of stories is that they build interpretations around social behavior. They tell us, in effect, "Here is a potentially problematic action that becomes quite sensible within this set of circumstances." We know that acts and situations are not static; they develop together and shape one another. Stories "develop" the relations between acts, actors, and situations from some point at which the action and the situation might have had multiple definitional possibilities to a point at which a dominant central action clearly establishes a significance for the situation and vice versa. This is what is often called the "point" of the story.

The listener's recognition of a central action and its development depends on various "bookkeeping" devices in stories. These regularities in story form organize information and enable listeners to make initial judgments about the story. For example, verb tense and pronoun usages in connection with commonsense understandings about action sequences provide for the serial development of action in stories. These usage rules include the consistency conventions pertaining to verb, noun, and pronoun references that help keep track of actors, actions, and relationships among actors. For example, we are constrained to introduce nouns in conjunction with pronoun references, and we must flag those that could refer to more than one noun. Pronoun-verb usages help clarify the point of view from which the action is being described. In short, these conventions help establish what happened, to whom, and when.

In addition to various grammatical conventions, stories employ assumptions about causal order and the linear sequence of action as aids to the identification of a central action and critical junctures in its development.[2] Newmark and Bloomfield illustrate how sequencing alone can distinguish a story (1) from a nonsensical collection of utterances (2):

1. Yesterday I was in this bar. The funniest thing happened. A lady walked in and asked for the manager in a loud voice. Well, he came over and asked what the trouble was. All she said was, "You Satan," and then she hit him over the head with her wet umbrella.
2. All she said was, "You Satan," and then she hit him over the head with her wet umbrella. Well he came over and asked what the trouble was. A lady walked in and asked for the manager in a loud voice. The funniest thing happened. Yesterday I was in this bar.[3]

Despite the incoherence of the second story, it is obvious that not all stories are told in linear fashion. This suggests the existence of other bookkeeping devices, such as causal cues or time lapses, that make it possible to tell stories with the aid of various plot devices like flashback, flash-forward, and multiple points of view.[4] For example, disjointed time references in the absence of causal cues make this an inadequate story: "Last week George went to Buffalo where he met, for the first time, Sally, his wife of ten years." The insertion of a causal qualifier can, however, repair the time warp and create an adequate story: "George and Sally had been pen pals for years. Although their occupations kept them apart, they became married in an unusual ceremony-by-correspondence. Last week, George went to Buffalo where he met, for the first time, Sally, his wife of ten years."

These and other story devices help the listener keep track of sequencing, climax, point of view, the emergence of new situational and behavioral factors, and possible changes in the relations between action and setting. These constraints on information in stories aid listeners in making their first essential judgment in the process of interpretation. By establishing consistent patterns of relationship between actions and situations, listeners can make calculated guesses about which actions in a story should be interpreted with reference to which specified conventions. These points are illustrated by Propp in his analysis of folktales. He argues that grammarlike conventions in storytelling alert the listener to connections between actions and scenic elements. The overall pattern of connections is organized around a central action that governs the point of the story. Propp does not, however, specify how these structural connections are interpreted or systematized.[5] These operations encompass the next two components of our model of stories and cognitive operations.

Interpreting the Central Action

After the listener has identified a candidate for a central action in a story, the relations between the action and the surrounding situational elements must be established. The point of the story emerges from these relations. As mentioned above, the grammatical, temporal, and causal regularities in story form set up obvious connections among pairs or clusters of symbols in a story. These structural connections guide the process of substantive interpretation. The listener searches among connected symbols to find ones that jointly support a probable interpretation of the story's central action. These isolated interpretations, in turn, further establish the precise relationship between the central action and its surroundings. In other words, there is a sort of "symbolic triangulation" at work in which certain symbols are placed in structural proximity, their mutual relationships are established in light of the central action, and these relationships in turn clarify the general significance of the central action.

This process of providing an interpretation for a body of information as new pieces of information are added has been demonstrated in experiments conducted by Garfinkel and Cicourel.[6]

What these studies suggest for our perspective is that triangulation occurs as the interpreter shifts among the information or sets of symbols that have been assimilated, the emerging idea that seems to be the point of the story, and new bits of information or groups of symbols. The emerging set of connections and constraints guides the listener's use of the vast store of background knowledge about social life that is necessary for sensible interpretation. The inferences that fill in the framework of connections among story symbols are based on various types of background understandings that can enter into the interpretation of social action: empirical knowledge, language categorization, logical operations, norms, and aesthetic criteria. As the following overview indicates, each of these types of background knowledge can serve as a powerful means of drawing inferences around a story's central action.

Empirical Connections. In many cases an empirical understanding may provide the key connection in an interpretation. Let's return to our hypothetical poisoning case. We have determined beyond a reasonable doubt that the victim was poisoned and that the cause of death was rat poison mixed with hot chocolate. In other words, we know that the act was murder and we know how it was done. A chain of circumstances leads us to believe that the husband must have committed the action. Imagine, however, that the neighbor testified that his vantage point on the night of the crime allowed him to see more than just the garage door. He also saw into the house. After the defendant entered the house he went to the kitchen. He made a hot drink in a mug and added some of the rat poison to it. He then left the kitchen and reappeared a few moments later in the upstairs bedroom. He gave the mug to the woman in bed and sat beside her as she drank it. This empirical connection between surrounding story elements and a clearly specified central action removes all doubt from the case.

Empirical connections often become important in cases that turn on a conflict between the accounts of the defendant and the only eyewitness. The interpretation of these cases may depend on locating subtle inconsistencies in the empirical connections of the two contending stories. These empirical inconsistencies may include the concurrence of improbable or impossible events, incorrect statements about causality, distorted connections between time and action, or the unexplained transformation of key scenic or behavioral symbols.

Consider an empirical understanding that became important to the interpretation of the central action in a larceny case.[7] We know that it can happen that a car being driven down a street can stop, the driver can slide over into the passenger's seat, and a waiting pedestrian can take the driver's place and drive off. This familiar scenario was important to the defendant's story, but a gap in the order of events in the scenario inhibited empirical connections that would have favored the defendant's interpretation. An eyewitness identified the defendant as the man who put a stolen stereo set in a hiding place across the street from her house. The man then ran around the corner, and she went to call the police. The defendant later took the stand and said that he had been at the scene but that he wasn't the man who hid the stereo set. He was just walking along when he saw another guy from the neighborhood (he thought his name was J___) carrying a stereo set. Suddenly a police car making its rounds came into sight, and J___ put the stereo in a nearby garbage can and ran off. What, then, happened to the defendant? He claimed that he hid under a nearby porch until the excitement died down. He had a prior arrest record and did not want to get involved in this matter. What became of the man who ran off? Why wasn't he found anywhere in the neighborhood later? According to the defendant as he pointed to a diagram of the scene, "a car came by here. The guy instead of getting into a car, he got right under the wheel and drove away."

He left something out here. Did the car come to a stop? Did the driver slide over so J___ could drive the car? Was there a driver? The judge who ruled on the case took note of these problems in the defendant's account of this otherwise familiar situation. Among the reasons cited for finding the defendant guilty was the following:

I believe I understood also that your testimony was that when you came out from under the D——— house you saw J——— I think further north on the same block emerge running from between some houses and jump into that car, into the driver's seat. That struck me as being unusual, that a man who was running from a burglary would jump into the driver's seat of a car that was moving and waiting for him.

This suggests a listener's maxim in situations, like adjudications, that require empirical judgments to be made about accounts: descriptions are taken literally. Terms that would have to be changed to produce a sensible version of an incident are regarded as problematic. They become possible indicators of "made up" versions of reality.

Language Category Connections. Language categories are among the most powerful means of establishing relationships among symbols in stories. Most symbols belong to multiple categories of possible usage. We can narrow the categorical relationship between symbols by locating the set of categories that could include the connected symbolic terms, and then determining the category that best explains the usage in the story context. In his excellent discussion of categorization, Sacks analyzed the simple child's story, "The baby cried. The mommy picked it up."[8] Sacks claimed that virtually all hearers of this story will understand that the mommy is the mommy of the baby. This is because of all the categories that could have been used to connect the symbols ("family," "stage of life," "sex," etc.) the category that makes most sense in the context of the story is "family." Consequently we understand that the two actors are related even though we have not been explicitly instructed to hear this. Sacks drew from this another "hearer's maxim" in interpretation: if a categorization permits the hearer (we prefer "listener") to draw a clear and sensible inference about the connection between the categorized symbols, the listener will make that categorical connection.[9]

Schank and Abelson's work on scripts illustrates this general maxim. Scripts classify a whole set of related activites in a single category. Once a script has been invoked, all the activities classified under that script will be invoked also. The restaurant script, for example, includes looking at a menu, ordering, being served, eating, paying the bill, and so on. Going to a restaurant for dinner implies all of these activities. Once a script has been invoked, unless told otherwise one can use the script categorization to interpret other statements. Thus, the story, "John went to the restaurant. He ate a lobster dinner," will be interpreted to mean that John ate lobster at the restaurant referred to in the previous statement. In other words, the category in which it makes most sense to interpret these sentences (and the categorization that, in fact, makes these statements interpretable) is established by the restaurant script.[10]

A categorization can become the key link in establishing a chain of connections to the central action in a story. An example of this emerged during the testimony in a burglary trial in our sample of cases. The defendant's mother was called to testify as a witness for the prosecution. She was asked if she knew the whereabouts of her son on the day of the crime. She said that she did not know what he was doing. The prosecutor then asked her if she hadn't agreed to sign a statement shortly after the burglary that clearly implicated her son in the crime, but refused to sign the statement after her son talked her out of it. The woman replied that she had thought the statement in question referred to a friend of hers, a Mr. P____, who had been arrested about the same time as her son. She said the statement seemed to fit what she knew about the incident and she was about to sign it when her son arrived at the prosecutor's office, read the statement, and pointed out to her that the statement was about him and not about Mr. P____. Since the woman didn't know anything about her son's case, she couldn't sign the statement.

This is a fascinating categorization problem. Did the woman refuse to sign the statement at the last moment to protect her son, or was her refusal, as she claimed, a response to discovering that the statement was about the wrong person? In order to make this judgment about the central action, we must rely on our knowledge about categorization, and we must also make a categorization. First, we use our knowledge about categorization to determine whether a person who knew two "arrested persons" (category) would identify (categorize) the wrong one in a prosecutor's statement. We know implicitly that categorization allows us to make both subtle distinctions and powerful generalizations about the world. It is not likely that a person who knew the details of two arrests could not distinguish between them when hearing an account of one of them. This would be similar to knowing that mothers and their babies belong to the category "family," but not knowing that they can be distinguished according to other sorts of categories (size, age, behavior, etc.). Yet this failure to make distinctions is what the woman claimed in response to the prosecutor's questions:

Q: Did I read you a statement after I interviewed you?
A: Yes . . .
Q: Did I ask you if it was true, if it was correct?
A: Yes. I said that because I thought it was Mr. P____. I am trying to tell you that now.
Q: You told me that the statement was correct that I read you?
A: Yes. I was mistaken.
. . . .
Q: And didn't your son appear at my office door at that time and walk you down to the bathroom?
A: Yes. I had the wrong thing—I was talking about the wrong date.
Q: Your son told you that—
A: When he got arrested—when Mr. P____ got arrested. It was Mr. P____.
Q: Is that what your son told you?
A: That's what I found out today. I didn't know.
. . . .
Q: Didn't your son object to your signing it?
A: Because I had the wrong date. If I had the right date, he would have let me sign it.
. . . .

Q: How did you know the statement was not accurate?
A: He heard me say what time it was and what date. That's why he stopped me. He said "You're talking about Mr. P____ there." I didn't know.

Notice here that if we decide that this failure to categorize properly was unlikely under the circumstances, we probably buttress this conclusion on the basis of a categorization we have made about the actors involved. It is not incidental to our judgment that the key actors in the situation are mother and son. We understand that the "family" category is the appropriate one to use even though many other categories could be invoked to describe the relationship between the actors (age, sex, race, religion, etc.). Thinking of the characters in the story as mother and son increases the chance of considering that mothers often act to protect their children when they are in trouble. This empirical knowledge can be called up more directly through the category "family" than through such categories as age, sex, or religion.

Consider in this light the prosecutor's repeated references in his questions to the woman's "son": "And didn't your *son* appear?" "Didn't your *son* object?" The prosecutor did not refer to the male actor in the story as "the man," "the defendant," "the accused," "the person who came to the door," or "Mr. Smith." These references would have been awkward in the context of the story. They would have strained against connections in the story that would establish the most obvious interpretation for the story's main action (the woman's refusal to sign the statement against her son). It makes sense to combine what we know about the relationship between the actors in the story to draw the inference that the mother probably refused to sign the statement to protect her son. From this we draw yet another listener's maxim pertaining to categorization to complement the one suggested by Sacks. To the extent that doubts (or choices) may exist as to the categorical relation between two story symbols, the interpreter will make the categorization that sets up the most obvious chain of connections between the symbols and the story's central action.

Logical Connections. When we combine empirical understandings with particular categorical operations, we produce "logic" in the everyday sense. This everyday logic is to be distinguished from formal logic, which may use artificial (nonnatural language) symbols and arbitrary rules of relationship among these symbols. The logic of ordinary discourse is based on the rules that govern everyday usage (grammar and semantics) and on the rules of empirical relationship that we know to hold in the everyday world. If, for example, we hear a story that begins, "We were waiting in the parking lot for our contact to deliver the drugs, and a car drove up," we also hear, among other things, that the engine of the car was running. Categorizing a car's action as "driving" presumes a variety of constituent (empirical and categorical) actions: engine running, wheels turning, and so on. This categorization also makes it possible to establish empirical connections to other "variables": speed, distance, and the like. We know these things by virtue of the set of symbols included by the categorical connection between "car" and "driving" and the invariant empirical relationships that connect these symbols. Thus, to modify our definition of everyday logic, we can say that a logical connection depends on categorizing two symbols such that some invariant empirical properties always accompany the categorization.

It happens that this apparently trivial example of the car and its engine became an issue in a narcotics case in our sample. The arresting officer testified that the defendant had driven to the scene of the arranged "buy" in the car containing the drugs. The defense attempted to weaken the connections between the actors, the agency, and the scene. For some curious reason the lawyer questioned the connection between the car and the scene of the crime. This was an attempt to test the credibility of the witness. Such efforts generally fail when they are aimed, as in this case, at unproblematic logical features of the witness's story:

Q: Was the motor of the Gremlin running?
A: I would assume so.
Q: Detective, I don't want you to assume anything that you don't have a fresh recollection of. Do you recall whether it was running or not?
A: I can't answer that question without assuming that it was.
Q: Well, maybe we can approach it another way. Why do you assume that it was running?
A: Because it drove up alongside.

To think other than this would be absurd. We know that a car cannot be driving and at the same time not have its engine running. We do understand logically that a car can be "coasting" or "rolling" and not have its engine running, but this sort of re-categorization would not make sense within the story.

Normative Connections. Categorizations and logical chains of inference can be supported by, or even based upon, normative understandings about excusable and inexcusable behavior in certain circumstances. Such normative understandings played a key role in establishing and testing the chain of connections leading to the jury's interpretations in the federal bank robbery trial of Patricia Hearst. The defendant had been an earlier kidnap victim of the group that staged the robbery. The defendant, however, entered the bank with her former abductors. Both sides agreed that she was carrying a gun. What did this behavior mean? Was she a willing participant? Had she come to identify with her former adversaries? If so, her acts conformed to the definition of robbery that was given to the jury. Or, on the other hand, had she been forced to participate in the robbery? Was she afraid for her life? If so, she was to be held less responsible for her actions. This is a normative judgment. It is also a case in which an initial categorization helps to establish the basis for the application of normative understandings about her actions.

Both sides agreed that the defendant had been kidnapped

earlier by the other robbers. The question was whether or not this categorical relationship still existed at the time of the robbery. The prosecution suggested that by the time of the bank robbery, the former victim had become a willing and loyal member of the group that had abducted her. Therefore, loyalty, and not threat or coercion, accounted for her participation in the robbery. The defense, however, sought to establish that the relationships that existed between the defendant and the other robbers sustained the categorization "kidnapping" throughout the relationship. The defendant took the stand and testified to numerous instances of physical abuse inflicted by her abductors. The defense argued that these episodes justified the conclusion that her participation in the robbery was secured through physical coercion. Therefore, she was entitled to be excused for her acts. The prosecution, however, proceeded to introduce other empirical connections into the relationship between the actors in the story. For example, the defendant stood regular guard watches while her "abductors" slept. She also went jogging alone during her period of "captivity." Once she became trapped while trying to climb a bluff near a beach. Two policemen assisted her. She did not inform them of her "plight." Finally, she waited alone in a getaway car (with the keys in the ignition) while two of her "abductors" robbed a store. The defendant even fired shots into the store to aid the escape.

The defendant was trying to establish a motive of threat or coercion for her participation in the crime. This motive, if accepted, would establish a normative connection between the act and the actor favorable to the defendant. The establishment of this motive would identify the defendant as the type of person who needed to be coerced into committing a crime rather than the type who would willingly commit a crime. This categorization, however, was valid only so long as it was evident that the defendant was using rules accepted by most members of the society to produce this interpretation. The incidents outlined by the prosecutor made it clear that the defendant was not using commonly accepted rules in achieving this interpretation. These incidents redefined the relationships among the actors from "adversaries" to "comrades." This redefinition relied on a powerful norm: if one is in a relationship against one's will, opportunities to escape the relationship should be exercised. This set of connections led the jury to the inference that the defendant acted in accord with her conscience while participating in the robbery.

The relationship between normative and categorical understandings might have changed had the defense presented a different case. Suppose that the defense had argued that the relationship between kidnappers and victim was more one of mind control than physical coercion. The kidnappers had effectively brainwashed their hapless victim. A new norm would emerge here as a basis for other categorical and empirical connections: persons who have been brainwashed should not be held accountable for their subsequent behavior. This understanding could have provided consistent connections for the defendant's numerous failures to escape her captors.[11]

This example suggests in graphic terms that issues of truth or fact in our adjudication (and social judgment) processes are intimately tied to the form and content of the stories in them. In some instances true accounts will be disbelieved because of improper definitions of terms or structurally inadequate presentations, and false accounts may be believed because of the skillful juxtaposition of internally consistent symbols. This example also illustrates the complementary use of multiple social understandings (empirical, categorical, normative) to build a solid interpretation.

Aesthetic Connections. Some definitions of story elements invite us to make connections that go beyond mere empirical, normative, categorical, or logical understandings. Some symbolic relationships seem somehow more acceptable, familiar, pleasing, or satisfying than others. These relationships may become targets for emotional release or personal identification. Other definitions may elicit connections that seem strange, awkward, unfamiliar, or even repulsive. We may invest negative feelings in these understandings. Both of these kinds of connections fall in the realm of aesthetics: relationships among symbols based on emotionally arousing ascriptive characteristics.

It is obvious that jurors are bombarded by lawyers with invitations to stereotype defendants, victims, and witnesses. These invitations are, in effect, pressures for jurors to make connections that are, perhaps, satisfying, familiar, or pleasing—connections that may be stronger than the facts, norms, or logic of the matter would suggest. Consider, for example, the defense lawyer's efforts to create an unsavory picture of the victim in a robbery case. It was established that the victim worked as a commercial fisherman. He had been at sea for several months, and he was celebrating his homecoming with his niece and his daughter on the night he was robbed. The celebration was unplanned. The two women had come from another city to visit the man. They went to the boat on which he lived. He was not there. They began checking local taverns and found him in one of them. From there the party moved from bar to bar until the man's wallet was stolen as the threesome was in transit between bars. These are the facts of the victim's whereabouts that evening. In the following list of defense questions, notice how the phrasing characterizes the victim in terms that might elicit more than just empirical, normative, logical, or categorical connections to other elements in the story:

Q: Now, if you just wanted to socialize with these two relatives of yours, wouldn't it have been easier to go to their home and socialize as opposed to drinking, wouldn't it have been easier to go to one of their houses rather than to the N____ Tavern, the B____ Tavern, and the E____ Club for a period of some five hours?

. . . .

Q: But you did your socializing in bars and taverns?

. . . .

Q: Did they just show up at the N____ Tavern?

. . . .

Q: And you happened to be there?

. . . .

Q: Just a coincidence?

. . . .

Q: You happened to be at the N____ Tavern when your daughter and niece were there?

. . . .

Q: No plans were made?

. . . .

Q: They just showed up and came in from Sea-Tac and just showed up at the N____ Tavern where you were?

In this case the verdict was against the defendant, so any stereotypes that may have been formed from this exchange did not carry the day. However, the power of aesthetic patterns in judgment may be much greater in instances such as the prosecution story about the defendant in this case. It was established that the defendant worked as a prostitute. The prosecutor developed a good deal of his case around questions about her life on the streets, her association with pimps, her use of drugs, and her use of weapons. The general picture that emerged about this person strained in the direction of making inferences consistent with a definition of her actions as "robbery," even when solid empirical or categorical bases for such connections were weak.

Evaluating the Interpretation of a Story

As suggested earlier, the story form facilitates more than just the recognition of a central action and the connection of relevant symbols in support of an interpretation. The listener must be able to refine constantly the conception of the central action and to compare it to emerging alternative candidates for the point of the story. More important, the listener must be able to know implicitly when enough connections have been established to make a consistent and confident interpretation. Related to this, the interpreter also must know what particular bits of information are needed to complete a story if it is found lacking. These interpretive abilities associated with storytelling indicate that stories must engage some general cognitive models of social action against which particular networks of story connections can be judged for completeness, consistency, and ambiguity.

A good candidate for this third cognitive component of the story model is Burke's "pentad" of social action elements.[12] The five elements of scene, act, agent, agency, and purpose provide the framework for a statement from which one can judge both completeness and consistency. According to Burke, we systematize information about social action in terms of the basic relations among these five elements. This social "frame" gives us a ready standard against which to compare an emerging interpretation, and through which to identify quickly any connection that appears to deviate from the empirical, categorical, and other ratios ordinarily associated with the comparison frame. This idea of general frames of reference within which interpretations can be crystallized, tested, and rearranged has become a central construct in cognitive sociology and cognitive psychology.[13] Frames are thought to impose generic attributes on specific data. The capacity of frames to impose a systematic structure on complex information sets accounts for the great speed, flexibility, and information capacity of ordinary interpretation. Frames make it unnecessary to reconstruct images that already have been assembled and stored in memory. The appeal of Burke's scheme is that it actually specifies the structure of the frames we apply to social interpretation. Data from trials in our sample suggest that Burke's model makes a good deal of sense. The basic elements of scene, act, agent, agency, and purpose seem to operate as "supercategories" into which multiple connections among symbols can be collapsed, and through which quick access to alternative symbolizations can be obtained.

The use of implicit ratios among elements in Burke's frame to generate and test alternative patterns of connections among story symbols is particularly obvious in the consistency tests that lawyers and jurors apply to emerging interpretations of stories. It is often the case in a complex trial that isolated connections among story symbols make sense, but the overall pattern of connections is inconsistent. An interesting example of this came up in a narcotics trial. At one point in the development of the case, the central question boiled down to whether the defendant had been duped into driving the car containing the narcotics to the scene of the drug sale, or whether he was in league with the person who arranged the sale. It was an uncontested fact that the defendant met the drug dealer in a bar before the sale. The defendant, however, claimed that he knew the dealer only slightly and certainly not well enough to know that he was a dealer. The defendant explained his presence in the bar by saying that his car had broken down nearby and he was trying to figure out how to get home to pick up his tools. After an hour or more, this other fellow walked in. He offered the defendant the loan of his car if the defendant would drop him off at a nearby shopping center (the scene of the deal) and return for him later. It was upon his return that the defendant was arrested.

This explanation gave the defendant a plausible purpose for acting as the driver of the car. (The car was the agency for his action.) How was he to know that there were drugs in a car that he had borrowed? These favorable connections between "agent-purpose" and "agent-agency" were, however, later shown to be inconsistent with another symbol added to the story when the prosecutor cross-examined the defendant. It turned out that the bar in which the defendant encountered the drug dealer was only a few blocks from his home. Why, the prosecutor asked, didn't he just walk home to get his tools instead of going to such elaborate lengths and wasting so much time? When we consider this scenic element, the formerly consistent connections suddenly become inconsistent. The triads with agent and scene as elements now show inconsistencies because of the change in scene (agent–purpose–scene; agent–agency–scene). In this fashion, the basic structure of a story can trigger a large number of structural permutations with which to test the consistency of connections that, taken in pairs, might seem perfectly consistent.

Stories, Judgments, and Reality

This theory of stories and social judgment explains how ordinary persons can make sophisticated judgments about complex information—even in situations, like the courtroom, in which there are few familiar formal cues to guide the process. The model also suggests how basic storytelling processes can be accommodated within the symbolic framework of a specialized situation like a trial. In the courtroom, for example, jurors must understand that their judgments should satisfy standards of "reasonable doubt." They must try to withhold final judgments until "all the evidence is in." They must try to be "fair." They must try to be "objective." [14] These official characteristics of good legal judgments are phrased in terms of symbols of law and justice, yet the judgments themselves are not the products of special legal knowledge or unique justice routines. Legal judgments must emerge from the juror's everyday cognitive repertoire. This raises an important question. If legal judgments are produced by everyday storytelling operations, how do these operations become labeled in terms of the characteristics of legal judgments? Something about story operations must correspond to the implicit criteria for doing justice. For example, particular story operations allow the juror to know whether an inference is based on a set of connections that are internally consistent and that yield no other interpretations. This, in a nutshell, is our everyday measure of "doubt." In a like manner, the assessment for story completeness tells the juror whether or not more information of a particular sort would yield a better interpretation. The very process of building an interpretation by working back and forth among the three cognitive operations and testing the result against the other side's story is what we mean ordinarily by being objective and fair.

Does all this mean that jurors' judgments (and most other social judgments as well) are based on objective pictures of what "really" happened? Not at all. At every stage of the storytelling-interpretation process, both storytellers and interpreters make choices about how to define story elements, and what frames of reference to apply. In this sense, a story is a reconstruction of an event in light of the teller's initial perception, immediate judgments about the audience, the interests that appear to be at stake, and, perhaps most important, what has gone before in the situation in which the story is presented. Likewise, the juror's judgment depends on all of these factors, in addition to his or her basic interpretive ability (command of language, general knowledge, etc.), assessment of the situation, and perception of the intentions of the storyteller.

As explained in Chapter 2, the symbolic representations on which verdicts are based may have little to do with what "really" happened in a dispute. Although justice processes are allegedly designed for the impartial determination of issues of fact, our perspective suggests that adjudicators, like most other story audiences, judge the plausibility of a story according to certain structural relations among chosen symbols, not according to direct perception of the actual events in question. Although documentary evidence exists to support some symbolizations in a story, both the teller and the interpreter of the story *always* have some margin of control over the definition of certain key symbols.

As we have seen, the stories that trial participants construct represent capsule versions of reality. In the process of taking incidents from one social context and placing them in another, the actor selects data, specifies the historical frame, redefines situational factors, and suggests missing observations.[15] In short, he or she can re-present an episode in a version that conforms with his or her perspective both during and after the incident. This does not mean that the storytellers have complete freedom to create reality. It simply reflects the importance of the choice of symbols and the structure of the relations among them in a story format. The importance of these factors is documented in the next chapter.

Chapter 4

Truth and the Structure
of Social Judgment

The importance of story structure stems from the fact that most social action is problematic. Almost any act can be associated with diverse causes, effects, and meanings. As pointed out in Chapter 3, a person who delivers narcotics to the scene of a drug sale could be regarded as a criminal engaged in an illegal activity, or as an innocent dupe who had been deceived about the nature of his errand by the narcotics pusher. A president who withholds pertinent information from federal investigators could be upholding the mandates of the Constitution pertaining to his office, or he could be trying to avoid justifiable criminal prosecution. One news story about a political speech may treat the substance of the speech as its key feature, while another may highlight the audience reaction to the speaker. One sports analyst may explain the success of a key play in a football game in terms of a defensive miscue, while another may point to a brilliant offensive move.

In addition to having the potential for multiple significance, social actions are so complex that exhaustive descriptions are impossible. There is simply too much information surrounding any action to permit "complete" description. Most important, the meaning of an action has little or no connection to the sheer quantity of detail in accounts about it. Constructing an interpretation for a problematic social action of the sort that lies at the center of most legal disputes requires the use of some communications device that simplifies the natural event, selects out a set of information about it, symbolizes the information in some way, and organizes it so that the adjudicators can make an unambiguous interpretation and judge its validity. Stories are the most elegant and widely used communication devices for these purposes. In Chapter 3 we suggested that stories contain a set of structural properties that serve as guides to the audience in:

1. Locating the central action that is to be explained by the story.
2. Connecting the various symbols in the story through the use of interpretive rules that establish the relations among the supporting information surrounding the central action. These rules consist of empirical, categorical, logical, normative, and aesthetic understandings that are triggered by the presence of particular symbols in the context of the story.
3. Evaluating the connections for internal consistency, completeness, and their collective implication for the central action.

This does not mean that evidence or information is of no consequence in judging stories. Nor does this perspective imply that the "judgments of fact" made about stories in many legal settings are based purely on the structural properties of stories. We cannot, however, ignore the fact that even "facts" are symbolized, and that there always exists some degree of choice over the symbols assigned to the various facts in an account. Moreover, inferences about action must always be based on implicit connections among symbolized facts or information. These connections must be suggested by communicators or provided by audiences. Finally, the collection of symbols and their interconnections must be interpreted according to the conventions associated with the communications device: the story. The transformation of events into story form imposes certain constraints on the types of symbols that can be assigned together, the connections that can be drawn between various symbols, and the features of a situation that have to be symbolized to produce a complete and interpretable account. In other words, the structure of a story can be just as important as its documentation. Although it is doubtful that completely undocumented stories will be believed in many instances, it is quite possible that adequately documented but poorly structured accounts will be rejected because they do not withstand careful scrutiny within a story framework. Similarly, a well-constructed story may sway judgments even when evidence is in short supply.

It is also important to consider that since most audiences for stories (e.g., jurors) have not been directly exposed to the events or actions in them, they have little recourse but to base their judgments about the credibility of stories on assessments about story structure. These assessments involve either applying interpretive rules to story symbols to connect them to a common theme, or fitting the set of connections in the story into some "frame" or model of social action (such as Burke's pentad) to determine the consistency and completeness of the network of connections as it bears on the central action in the story. To the extent that these assessments yield ambiguities, the story will be both difficult to interpret and regarded as implausible. Ambiguities may result from several sources. Key symbols in a story may be impossible to relate if workable interpretive rules cannot be located to connect them. In other cases, interpretive rules may suggest too many possible relationships between key symbols. They may make the precise role of the symbols in the story impossible to determine. In still other cases, the role of a symbol in a story may be rendered ambiguous because its obvious relations with other symbols are inconsistent with prior connections that were in keeping with the story line.

If the theory is correct, the frequency of these structural ambiguities in a story should have several effects on judgment. The higher the frequency of ambiguities, the more difficult it will be to interpret the central action, or the point, of the story. The higher the frequency of ambiguities, the more variation there will be in the interpretations of those members of the audience who do make sense of the story (since they will have to bring more of their own creative resources to the judgment task). Finally, as the number of ambiguities increases, the chance that the audience will accept the story as it stands as plausible or true decreases.

The last of these hypotheses concerning story structure and the truth status of stories addresses the crucial issue in adjudication proceedings: whether there are any intrinsic characteristics of true stories that enable people to recognize them as true, or whether the perceived truth or falsity of stories is a function of their symbolic structures. In order to isolate the variables affecting judgments about stories, we decided to analyse simple social stories in controlled situations. We moved our research outside of the courtroom and away from a specific focus on legal questions so that we could study the general characteristics of story structure and judgment. We set up an experiment in which people told stories about their own experiences to an audience who judged whether the stories were true or false.

The research design (described below) that we employed in this investigation was sensitive to two related questions. First, we were interested to know whether audience judgments about the truth or falsity of a story (under conditions in which the audience had no independent check on the story) would be independent of the actual truth. The structural model predicts that, other things being equal, there will, under conditions of limited independent information, be no association between the inferred truth status and the actual truth status of a story.[1] Second, we were interested to know whether we could predict audience guesses about the truth of stories from the frequency of ambiguities in the stories. Even though there is nothing about the nature of truth that reveals itself in the structure of communication, the model predicts that particular structural properties of stories can lead audiences to *think* that they are true.

Subjects and Procedure

The subjects in this experiment were eighty-five undergraduate students in three political science classes at the University of Washington. They had never been exposed to the general theoretical perspective on storytelling, and they agreed to participate in the experiment with the understanding that it would be explained afterward. All the subjects were told that they might be called upon to tell a short story to the class. The pool of potential storytellers was divided randomly into two groups based on the last digit of their student identification numbers. The "odds" were instructed to compose a "false" story—that is, a story in which they were characters but that described something that had never happened to them or something they had not done. The "evens" were instructed to compose a "true" story—that is, a story about something that had happened to them or that they had done. All stories were to have the teller as a main character.

A total of forty-nine storytellers (chosen at random from the general pool) told their stories to the classes; forty-seven of these stories were suitable for analysis. Each storyteller became a member of the audience when not telling a story.[2] Since we were interested only in the impact of story structure on audience judgment, we did not permit audience members to question the storytellers about their stories. We also asked those who knew the storyteller well enough to be able to bring independent information to bear on their judgment to disqualify themselves from judging that particular story.

Each story was videotaped for purposes of analysis and assigned a number by the investigator. The audience members recorded the number of each story and recorded their judgment about the truth status of the story next to the number. The storytellers recorded the truth status of their stories on slips of paper and handed them to the investigator immediately after telling their stories. These data were coded and analyzed according to the procedures outlined below.

Analytical Procedures

We determined whether audience judgments varied independently of the truth status of the story simply by comparing audience guesses to each storyteller's claim about his or her story. The results of this comparison are presented and discussed in the next section. The second and more important question about the relation between story structure and the pattern of audience judgment required a fairly complex coding scheme for the stories. In the interests of explaining our results and encouraging further analytical use of the model, we will review this coding scheme. We began by operationalizing the concept of ambiguities in story structure, and then we developed a weighting scheme that gave more importance to those ambiguities that most directly inhibited the interpretation of the central action in a story.

Following the schema explained in Chapter 3, we screened each story for ambiguities of three types. First, ambiguities can occur when an obvious interpretive rule (fact, language category, norm, etc.) cannot be located to provide a sensible connection between two story elements. Second, the interpreter may see many possible connections between the symbols, but may not be able to select among them either because the symbols are poorly keyed to the rest of the story or because some intervening symbol (that would have clarified the relationship) has been omitted. Finally, ambiguities can result when the interpreter makes a sensible and unambiguous connection only to discover that it is inconsistent with the most obvious connections among other symbols in the story.

Since stories can vary tremendously in length and amount of detail, some symbols may be minor and distant from the central action while others may be of major importance and closely related to the central action. Ambiguities in relations among peripheral symbols will cause less interpretive difficulty than ambiguities in relations among symbols that bear directly on the central action of the story. This suggests that ambiguities nearest the central action should be weighted more heavily than other ambiguities.[3]

Finally, and, again, since stories vary in length and detail, our measure of structural ambiguity had to be standardized. Our assumption here is that a small number of ambiguities in a very short or simple story should cause a greater disruption in interpretation than a small number of ambiguities in a long and detailed story. The standardization of ambiguities based on the complexity of the story can be accomplished by weighting the number of ambiguous connections by the total number of connections among symbols in the story:

$$\frac{\text{number of ambiguous connections in entire story}}{\text{total number of connections in story}} + \frac{\text{number of ambiguous connections to central action}}{\text{total number of connections to central action}}$$

Our theory predicts that this measure will be inversely related to story credibility. The hypothesis is that as structural ambiguity increases, story credibility decreases. With the basic model in place we next faced the question of how to determine the connections and the ambiguities that the audiences would be most likely to find in these stories. Up to this point the model of story structure seems to have operated on the gross assumption that all stories will elicit the same connections and the same perceptions about ambiguity from all members of an audience. This is clearly not a viable assumption. Some stories may require special knowledge to be interpreted. For example, whether a story about a skiing accident is believed or disbelieved may depend on the skiing knowledge and vocabulary of each member of the audience. Such knowledge and jargon constitute an expanded set of interpretive rules. A more general statement of this observation is that for virtually any story different audience members will possess somewhat different interpretive skills (i.e., they will have different ranges of interpretive rules). Thus, the judgments about any story will be a product of the interaction between the symbolic form of the story and the interpretive capacity of the audience.

This "audience variance" problem was one that we had to confront if we were to use the structural model in a meaningful fashion. We clearly had the option of ignoring the problem since it could only bias the results of our investigation against our hypotheses by virtue of the fact that it would represent a massive source of random error in coding, and would, thereby, wash out any real pattern that might exist in the data. On the other hand, it would be absurd to assume that all interpreters possess the same set of rules, and it would have been silly to handicap our results by permitting such a large source of random error to go unchecked. Our study design and our coding procedures contained three precautions against the entry of too much of this error into our data.

First, the stories told in the experiment were all of the form "things that people do" or "things that can happen to people." This means that the stories dealt with general human interest topics. Such topics are among those most likely to elicit common understandings and interpretations. This is even more likely within this experiment since the subjects, being college students, were all fairly similar in age, social background, and immediate social circumstances.

Second, we decided to invoke in our coding procedure an analytical rule that is common to validation procedures in most language analysis disciplines. This rule might be called the "what any competent member knows" rule. For example, linguists validate deep grammar rules on the basis of judgments about whether they can be used to generate "grammatical" utterances in the language. Grammatical utterances are those that are understood as such by any competent member of the language community. Our version of the "what any competent member knows" rule involved making judgments about whether average members of an audience (more specifically, the audiences in our experiments) would possess the sort of interpretive rules necessary to make unambiguous connections among various story symbols.

Third, judgments about ambiguous connections among story elements were simplified by dividing the stories into three categories. The first category included accounts of events of which everyone would have some knowledge. Examples of these in our sample are stories about going to a birthday party and walking in the rain. The second category included accounts of events with which a large portion but not all of the audience would be acquainted. These included stories about rock climbing, skiing, and traveling. The third category included stories about subjects with which very few in the audience would have any acquaintance. Examples were stories about flying a helicopter in Vietnam and being a paratrooper. (Most stories fell in the first two categories.)

Recent research on social judgment and interpretation indicates that people tend to explain away ambiguities where possible. This research, on the whole, has been done using accounts of events that are very familiar to the listener. The subject matter of Garfinkel's research, for example, involved a personal problem of the person who was doing the interpreting.[4] Schank and Abelson, similarly, use events, such as going to a restaurant, that most people in this society readily understand.[5] The argument that these studies support is that when people know the information that either fills in a gap between elements of a story or produces consistency in elements that otherwise seem inconsistent, they will make use of this knowledge. Therefore, we reasoned that when the audience was capable of using everyday knowledge to interpret the story in a less ambiguous fashion, it would. Thus, it was relatively more difficult for a story in the first category to be labeled ambiguous than for a story in the third category. We will know more about these relationships as more research in this area accumulates.

Each story was diagrammed and scored for ambiguities by each author. After the independent coding was completed, the results were compared. Considering the complexity of the coding task the coder reliability was satisfactory. Reliability was upward of 80 percent agreement on all the various aspects of the coding task (identification of key story symbols, identification of the central action, the location of connections, the total number of connections, and the location and number of ambiguities). In cases of disagreement, each author presented the rationale for a particular coding. Most often this rationale came in the form of a confidence estimate abut the existence of an interpretive rule necessary to make a connection. Occasionally the debate would focus on the central action. (When there was disagreement about the central action, we usually found that the story as a whole was poorly structured.) Each author "won" about an equal number of these disagreements, and in almost every case the final coding was regarded as superior to the discrepant coder's original coding.

Two examples of actual stories should make our coding procedures, our structural diagrams, and the "operational logic" of our model clear. Although we could have selected any of the forty-seven stories for this illustration, the two we have chosen nicely illustrate the important point that the plausibility of stories has little to do with either their actual truth status or their structural complexity (length, number of elements, number of connections to the central action, etc.). The first story (entitled "The Birthday Party" by its teller) is a very simple, short, true story that was not believed by the majority of the audience. The second story (called "The Helo Story" by its teller) is a comparatively long, complex, false story that was overwhelmingly believed by the audience.

The Birthday Party

Ummm—last night I was invited to a birthday party for a friend her name's Peggy Sweney it was her twenty-fourth birthday. At the party we had this just suuuper spaghetti dinner—you know—just great big hunks of meat and mushrooms and what not—a nice salad. And then for dessert we had a um cherry and blueberry um cheesecake. It was really good.

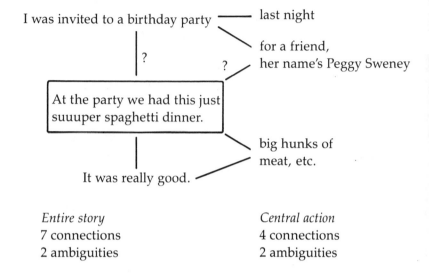

Figure 3. "The Birthday Party" Story Structure

The structural diagram of the story appears in Figure 3. The starting point of the diagramming process is to break the story down into structural elements (symbols and combinations of symbols) that have some bearing on the story's significance. The primary criterion for determining that a story phrase was a structural element was to ask whether or not it contained information that could be used to interpret another element in the story. For instance, the phrase "for a friend, her name's Peggy Sweney" helps give meaning to the phrase "I was invited to a birthday party," since going to a friend's birthday party is different from going to the birthday celebration of a famous acquaintance or of a store, city, or nation. This phrase could have been divided further with "her name's Peggy Sweney" separated from, but related to "for a friend." For example, this comment establishes the facts that his friend is a female and a person named Peggy Sweney. However, since the audience was not expected to recognize her name and since the fact that the friend is female did not seem potentially useful in the subsequent interpretation of the story, there was no reason to designate "her name's Peggy Sweney" as a separate structural element. If the audience had been the storyteller's close friends or family, if the sex of the actors had been significant to the point of the story, or if the name had been famous, the status of the phrase would have been different. Since none of these applied in this case, the phrase "for a friend her name's Peggy Sweney" was coded as one structural element. Following this general logic throughout the story we arrived at the six basic elements shown in Figure 3. When the structural elements were determined, lines were drawn between those elements that according to the interpretive rules would be connected.

In "The Birthday Party" a connection is made between "I was invited to a birthday party" and "At the party we had this just suuuper spaghetti dinner." Given the phrases contained in this story, these two are necessary for understanding one another. If the story had contained much more information, it is highly possible that these two phrases would not have been directly linked. We need some reference to a party before we can understand the meaning of what happened at the party. By itself the phrase "I was invited" is problematic: it is open to several interpretations. We cannot even state with certainty whether it is to be regarded as an action in the story or as a setting in which the story's action is to take place. More information in explanation of the phrase is required before it acquires any significance. Once the next element "At the party we had this just suuuper spaghetti dinner" is added, the first phrase is seen as part of the scene and the second as the action. At this point, we have sufficient information to call this group of phrases a story.[6] That is, we have our event (the party) and some constraining statements that permit interpretation.

The two phrases, "I was invited to a birthday party" and "At the party we had this just suuuper spaghetti dinner," have to be connected. Their connection, however, is ambiguous. This is indicated on the diagram by a question mark on the line between the two elements. The connection is ambiguous because there is some confusion about what the audience should understand about the dinner and the party. Eating supper is not inconsistent with going to a birthday party, but it is not necessarily the only thing that happens at a party. Nor is the act of eating a dinner a particularly unusual action—especially at a party. In short, any special significance it may have is not provided by the mere fact that it occurred at a birthday party. More information is needed for a clear interpretation to be possible. Without this information it is not clear why the dinner was mentioned, why it was the only event mentioned, or why it was so important. In short, the connection of these two elements seems to raise at least as many questions as it answers. This confusion is a defining characteristic of ambiguities in story structure. In terms of the Burkean pentad, the scene-agent ratio sets up a frame for an ordinary birthday party while the scene-act ratio develops the idea of a special dinner party. Though these two frames are not entirely inconsistent, they do not yield an unambiguous interpretation for the story.

Similarly the connection between "for a friend her name's Peggy Sweney" and "At the party we had this just suuuper spaghetti dinner" has a question mark on it. The phrase "for a friend" is a potential (or latent) explanation for what went on at the party (for example, Peggy may be a gourmet cook). In other words, given the position of this element in the story, its most likely function is to help connect the scene and the act. However, since we, as audience, know nothing about Peggy, the attempt to use this phrase to find the significance of eating dinner at the party is frustrated. In this case it was the teller's responsibility to provide clear instructions as to what information was contained in this element and how it should be used. It is not clear what facts, logic, norms, or the like, would yield a clear inference about the relationship between these story elements.

Other connections in this story need little explanation. "It was really good" describes the dinner and the dessert. Since "just great big hunks of meat" is another way of talking about the dinner, it is connected both to the "dinner" phrase and to the "really good" phrase. Neither of these connections is ambiguous. We can understand, and have no questions about, the relation of these elements.

"At the party we had this just suuuper spaghetti dinner" is enclosed in a box on the diagram. This indicates that it is the central action; it is the single most important element in the story structure. Designating one element as the central action is, in part, a subjective, interpretive process, as was the case with determining structural elements, drawing connecting lines, and pinpointing ambiguities. Nevertheless, we have been able to formulate several specific guidelines for finding the central action.

1. The central action must be an action.[7] Since the function of a story is to constrain a meaning for an action or event, the focal point of the story structure will be the action (or set of related acts) that is best developed by the surrounding structural elements. In general, the central action will be involved in more interpretive connections than other structural elements.
2. The central action should adequately answer the questions, What is the story about? and What is the storyteller trying to tell us?
3. The story will generally consist of a setting-concern-resolution sequence. The setting usually includes the time, the place, and some of the characters. The concern is an action that, given the setting, creates a climactic (eventful, ironical, suspenseful) situation. For example, if someone is rock climbing (as was the case in one of our stories) and he slips and falls, slipping and falling are the concern. If the story ended at this point, the audience would be left wondering: what happened to the climber? Was he hurt or killed? A complete story will provide an answer to these questions. This stage is the resolution. The central action is the structural element that creates the central question the story must resolve. The resolution normally resolves both the predicament created by the problem and the questions the listeners might have had about the outcome. In the rock-climbing story the resolution consisted of telling the audience that the climber was taken to the hospital for treatment. Note that "The

Birthday Party" does not have this characteristic setting-concern-resolution pattern. The next story we discuss ("The Helo Story") is, by contrast, one of the best examples of this construction.

"The Birthday Party" has a high percentage of ambiguous connections—particularly in relation to the central action. These ambiguities resulted primarily from the incompleteness of the story. The problems with interpreting "At the party" and "I was invited" and "At the party" and "for a friend" were not the result of inconsistencies among these elements. They were a consequence of structural gaps (missing elements) in places where the interpretive roles of the existing elements were in question.[8]

The second story we have diagrammed here is, by contrast, a good example of a tightly structured and unambiguous account:

The Helo Story

I was stationed in Vietnam as a helicopter pilot and flew reconnaissance missions, and about five weeks shy of an eighteen-month tour I was approximately three miles south of the DMZ and my oil pressure went down to about 6 *pounds* of a normal 180 pounds, and I had to put down—an' just—a helicopter's about the safest thing to land in 'cause you have a neutral rotor and you can just coast right down like a large parachute—from the time that I radioed in to the time that they picked me up just seemed like an *eternity*. As it was nothing happened—I got back to the base and read the report—it was a total of six minutes.

"The Helo Story" is an example of a story with no ambiguities. The agent (helicopter pilot flying reconnaissance missions) and the purpose ("oil pressure went down"—mechanical failure of helo) give the background information necessary to put the agent in a position where the act ("had to put down") was appropriate. The scene ("three miles south of the DMZ" and "five weeks shy of an eighteen-month tour" of duty) imbues the act with tension, and the agency (the safe-landing helicopter) specifies that the tension is a result *only* of the juxtaposition of scene and act. The meaning of the central action is well constrained both by the setting and by the resolution. Any audience reasonably aware of the Vietnam War (that is, having

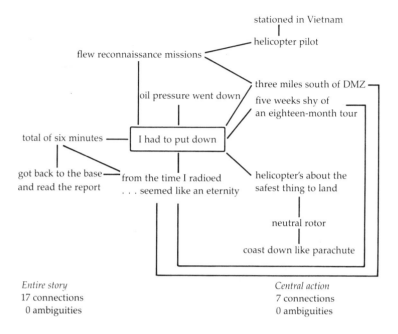

Figure 4. "The Helo Story" Story Structure

some sense of the danger of action near the DMZ or the ordeal of a tour of duty) would understand the anxiety or tension produced by having to put down three miles south of the demilitarized zone just five weeks before leaving Vietnam, and that this anxiety would make the wait seem like an eternity. Furthermore, the audience is instructed not to interpret the story as talking about the danger of a crash landing through the brief discussion of the landing mechanism of a helicopter. (An audience that knew something about helicopters might have paid more attention to this passage.)

The central action of this story has seven connections, all of which are easily understood. They are consistent with one another and with the central action. All of them give interpretive clues that support one interpretation and exclude all others.

(Contrast this with "The Birthday Party" which has four connections to the central action, two of which are ambiguous.) The very clear meaning of the central action is the major strength of "The Helo Story." It is reinforced by the lack of ambiguity among the other structural elements. Given the structural coherence of the story, it is not surprising that twenty-two out of twenty-nine audience members thought that the story was true. It happens to be false. The teller had never even been out of the country and had never been near a helicopter.

These two stories illustrate our diagramming technique. While they do not show the entire range of complexity we encountered, they do demonstrate all of the uses of the four basic constituents of the diagramming: *symbolic elements* in the stories, *connections* among them, *ambiguities* in the connections, and the relation of these connections and ambiguities to the *central action*. They also illustrate how the model in Chapter 3 informed the designation of elements, connections, and ambiguities. Stories of any degree of complexity can be diagrammed in similar fashion. The same components are always employed in the same ways. The number of elements, connections, and, usually, ambiguities increases in detailed stories, but their structural patterns remain the same.

Results

After all the stories had been coded in terms of their structural features, we were ready to test our two hypotheses. The reader will recall that these hypotheses, mentioned at the end of the first section of this chapter, were:

1. Audience judgments about the truth of the stories will be independent of the actual truth or falsity of the stories. If audiences must assess the truth of social stories in situations in which tellers are not generally bound to tell the truth, their guesses will be incorrect as often as they will be correct.
2. The pattern of audience guesses will be related to the structural

adequacy of stories. The greater the number of ambiguous connections in a story, and the closer these connections lie to the central action of the story, the greater is the probability that the story will be disbelieved.

The test of the first hypothesis is quite straightforward. We simply compared the actual status of each story with the audience guesses. Audience guesses were scored "correct" if a story was true and the number of true votes outnumbered false votes, or if a story was false and the false votes outnumbered true votes. Audience guesses about a story were scored "incorrect" if a story was true and the number of false votes outnumbered the true votes, or if a story was false and the number of true votes was greater than the number of false votes. Figure 5 displays the distribution of guesses in relation to the actual status of the stories.

As Figure 5 shows, more true stories were told than false ones. Part of this disparity may result from random error introduced by the method of assigning storytellers to the storytelling condition. It is also possible that some storytellers consciously reassigned themselves because they couldn't think of a false story. If such a shift occurred, it was relatively small (a maximum of five storytellers), and it should have worked against

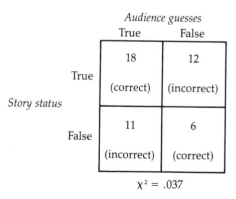

$$\chi^2 = .037$$

Figure 5. Audience Guesses Compared to Actual Status of Stories

our hypothesis, since tellers were choosing to tell stories they felt more comfortable telling. All of this aside, the results in Figure 5 show that the pattern of correct and incorrect guesses was essentially random. The chi square (X^2) statistic calculated for this table is only .037, indicating that the null hypothesis cannot be rejected, and that there is no statistical association between the actual truth status of stories and their perceived truth status.

We must be cautious in our interpretation of these findings. We do not imply here that there are no conditions under which the truth status of a story can be accurately determined. Various forms of documentary evidence in storytelling settings should increase the accuracy of guesses. However, our interest is in whether or not the simple structure of stories (independent of evidence) has an impact on judgment. To demonstrate this, we first must determine that there is nothing inherent in the nature of "true" or "false" stories that leads audiences to make correct judgments about truth status. We think the above data establish the conclusion that there is no intrinsic quality in true or false stories that telegraphs accurate impressions to interpreters. The next questions are whether or not there *is* a pattern to audience guesses, and whether or not structural properties of stories explain the pattern.

The relationship between structural ambiguity and credibility can be calculated easily from our data. Recall that we have already proposed a measure of story ambiguity. According to this measure, the ambiguity of a story is the result of the number of ambiguous connections in the entire story divided by the total connections in the story plus the number of ambiguous connections to the story's central action divided by the total number of connections to the central action. This measure controls for differences in length and complexity across stories, and it weights connections to the central action more heavily than peripheral connections. The next measure we needed to generate was a credibility score, or a measure of the degree to which each story was regarded as true by the interpreters. Ordinarily this would have been a simple matter of adding up the number of "true" votes assigned to each story. However, the stories were told in three sessions with different numbers of interpreters in each session. Since we pooled the data from the three groups, our credibility score had to standardize the audience guesses about each story.[9] We did this by weighting a measure of "true" guesses by the size of the audience. We also gave the score a convenient range of −1.0 to +1.0 by entering the number of "false" votes into the measure and making the difference between "true" votes and "false" votes a fraction of the total number of votes. The resulting credibility measure is: number of true votes minus number of false votes divided by total number of votes. A score of +1.0 meant that everyone in an audience believed that a story was true, and a score of −1.0 meant that no one in an audience believed that a story was true. We now can compare the distribution of credibility scores against the distribution of ambiguity scores from our model. The relationship between story structure and credibility is shown in Figure 6.

As the graph in Figure 6 shows, the structure of a story has a considerable impact on its credibility. Despite the rather high probability of error introduced into our coding by our inability to specify relationships among story variables with greater theoretical precision, the trend in the graph is both strong and in the predicted direction. The message is clear that as structural ambiguities in stories increase, credibility decreases, and vice versa.

The strength of the trend in Figure 6 can be demonstrated through several simple statistical tests and comparisons. The most obvious test is the strength of the correlation between structural ambiguity and story credibility. This correlation coefficient is −.407, and it is significant at the .01 level of confidence. This means that as the ambiguities in the symbolic structure of a story increase, the credibility of the story (as defined by the portion of people who regard it as true) decreases.

It is possible that a measure as complex as structural ambigu-

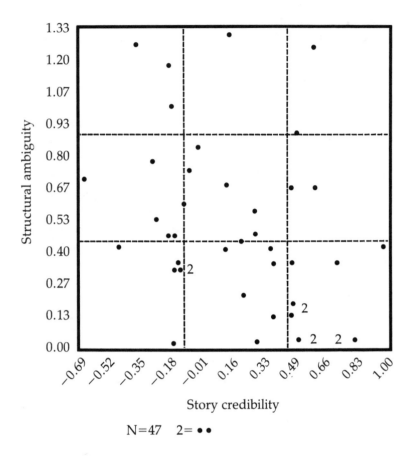

N=47   2= ● ●

Figure 6. Story Credibility as a Function of Structural
Ambiguity

ity may be masking the effects of other simpler variables in stories. For example, it is worth considering the possibility that the length of the story, the number of actions it contains, or the way in which it is told may have a great deal to do with the impact of a story on the judgments of interpreters. To assess the possible effects of other properties of stories, we measured some other structural and stylistic features of the stories in our sample. Although our measure of ambiguity controlled for the length and complexity of stories as defined by the number of inferential connections they require the interpreter to make, it is possible that the actual length in words affects listeners' judgments about credibility. It is also conceivable that the number of actions in a story might create complications leading to damaged credibility since part of the interpretation of a story requires distinguishing a central action from all the other actions. It is also important to consider the possibility that the style of the storyteller affects story credibility. Although there are any number of style variables that could be measured, the one that is at the same time most obvious and easiest to quantify is the degree to which the story delivery is halting and interrupted by pauses and lapses. We measured both the number of pauses in each story and their average length in seconds. Figure 7 compares

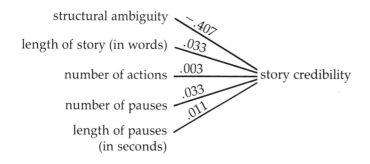

Figure 7. The Relationship of Structural Ambiguity and Other Variables to Story Credibility

NOTE: All figures are Pearson *r* correlation coefficients.

the effects on story credibility of our original ambiguity measure with the effects of measures of story length, number of actions in the story, number of pauses, and length of pauses.

   With the exception of the correlation between ambiguity and credibility, none of the other correlations is statistically significant at an acceptable level of confidence. Moreover, the relationship between ambiguity and credibility remains equally strong or becomes stronger when each of the other story variables is controlled. In other words, the predicted relationship between the symbolic structure of stories and story credibility holds true, and the strength of the relationship is not diminished by taking other story variables into account.

Discussion

The data reported above provide strong support for our hypothesis that, regardless of a story's actual truth status, the more ambiguous the story is in the structural terms we have specified, the less plausible it is. This is not to say that the relationship is a perfect one. The peripheral scatter among the points in Figure 6 may be the result of several factors. First and most important, our method of operationalization did not incorporate several distinctions that the model of story structure emphasized. For example, connections of all types were lumped together, even though the model specified meaningful theoretical differences between the types of connections (empirical, categorical, logical, normative, and aesthetic). Future research may also show that certain types of ambiguities should be weighted more heavily than others. We may have lost precision in estimating the strength of associations by not weighting in this way. It is, however, pointless to make such fine distinctions until we have more knowledge about them. Other measures, such as the relative impact of ambiguous connections as a function of their distance from the central action, could also be refined. Such refinements in the operationalization of the model would almost certainly increase the predictive capabilities of our empirical framework for the analysis of story structures. Factors outside the story structure may also influence credibility. Audience judgments may be affected by such disparate factors as the storyteller's personality, the number of stories that have already been told, the distractions in the environment, or even the time of day the stories are told. Finally, common sense tells us that some portion of the credibility variance will depend on a story's documentation. Nevertheless, the success of our operationalization, as demonstrated by the clear trend in the scatterplot, indicates that story structure is an essential explanatory variable in a key social judgment process.

The results of this experiment, as illustrated in Figures 5–7, unequivocally relate structural features of stories to credibility. These findings bear some significance for the study of story credibility and the uses of social stories. They tell us, quite simply, that the way in which a story is told will have considerable bearing on its perceived credibility regardless of the actual truth status of the story. This means that the symbols chosen, the structural elements (scene, act, agent, agency, and purpose) that are defined and left undefined, and the amount of detail provided to facilitate connections between story symbols, will all have a significant bearing on audience judgments about stories—judgments based on the overall completeness, consistency, and adequacy (in other words, the degree of ambiguity) of story connections.

These structural properties of stories become more important in two kinds of judgment situations. First, structural characteristics of stories become more central to judgment if facts or documentary evidence are absent. Such situations often occur, for example, in politics when leaders present accounts of political events to the general public. Second, the structure of stories becomes crucial to judgment in cases in which a collection of facts or evidence is subject to competing interpretations. In such cases, it may not be the evidence that sways final judgment; judgment hinges on the structure of interpretation that provides the best fit for the evidence. Most adjudication settings correspond to this latter type of situation. In trials, for example, jurors generally confront a body of undisputed evidence which has been contextualized within two competing stories about the crime (the central action) in dispute. The jurors know that both of the stories cannot be true, and their task is to find the one that assimilates the known facts more completely, more consistently, and with fewer problematic inferences. The "facts" in these and other storytelling situations may impose some limits on what a structurally adequate story can look like, but within these constraints there is a remarkable margin of freedom available for the symbolization of competing stories about the disputed action.

PART III
CREATING THE GROUNDS
FOR LEGAL JUDGMENT

Chapter 5
Case Construction Strategies in Trials

When one observes a trial it is hard to ignore the possibility (indeed, the probability) that cases are little more than highly stylized dramatizations of reality. In many trials, each side misses, or chooses to ignore, some potentially important aspect of the incident in question. It is common for lawyers to create the suspicion that key evidence in the opposition case is spurious or that it can be explained better in the context of a different web of circumstances than the one on which the opposition has based its case. It is clear from the patterns in opening and closing remarks and examination practices that both sides struggle to redefine facts consistently in the direction that best establishes their competing claims about the incident. These struggles over facts, definitions, and interpretations become the hard substance for judgment. In almost any trial there is the uneasy possibility that neither case captures the subtle reality of the incident.

If one operates under the misguided assumption that trials involve the straightforward presentation and testing of facts, it is virtually impossible to spot general patterns in the structure of cases or to identify basic prosecution and defense strategies that explain the significance of those patterns. If, however, trials are analyzed within a storytelling framework, it is easy both to see the patterns of case structure and to explain the strategies underlying cases. In fact, when cases are translated into storytelling practices, the strategies employed in case construction can be described by a surprisingly small set of categories.

The legal obligation of the prosecution to prove the guilt of the defendant beyond a reasonable doubt constitutes a clear strategic mandate for any prosecution case. All prosecution cases must attempt to construct a structurally complete story that constrains an internally consistent interpretation for the defendant's behavior. This means that prosecution cases must develop an action through a clear set of scenes, actors, agencies, and purposes that can be connected in support of the same interpretation of the defendant's behavior. The prosecution case cannot satisfy standards of reasonable doubt if it fails to define all of the structural story elements (scene, act, agent, agency, purpose) in terms that support the same meaning for the defendant's behavior.

In contrast to the fairly narrow strategic mandate that applies to prosecution cases, defense cases have a much wider array of strategic options. Since the defense need not prove the defendant's innocence, the strategy of constructing a complete story of its own is only one option. The defense has three general strategies that it can employ in response to the prosecution case. First, if the prosecution has not constructed a structurally complete or internally consistent story, the defense may choose to show merely that there are missing elements in the prosecution case or that the definitions of various scenes, acts, actors, agents, or purposes do not all support the same interpretation of the defendant's behavior. We call this the *challenge* strategy. If the prosecution case represents an adequate story in its own right, the defense may use a second strategy involving the redefinition of particular elements in the story to show that a different meaning emerges when slight changes are made in the interpretation of the evidence. We call this the *redefinition* strategy. In some cases the defense may find it difficult to challenge or reinterpret the prosecution story and, as a result, may elect to pursue a third strategy: to tell a story of its own. Under this third strategy the defense may introduce its own evidence in order to tell a completely different story about the defendant's behavior. We call this the *reconstruction* strategy. The selection of the most advantageous defense strategy depends on how well the prosecution has executed its strategic mandate.

The Prosecution Strategy

The judge's instructions at the end of a trial remind the jury of the prosecution's obligation to construct a structurally complete story. The general form of instructions serves as a sort of checklist with which to begin assembling the structure of the prosecution case:

In order to convict the defendant of the crime of _____, the state must prove to you beyond a reasonable doubt that:

(Actor) The said defendant _____
(Scene) did on the charged date/time/place/occasion, etc.
(Purpose) willfully/knowingly/with intent to do bodily harm, etc.
(Agency) use force/cause the victim fear of bodily harm/offer for sale/ use a false identification, etc.
(Act) to take the property of/to cause the death of/to deceive, etc.

In most trials, the instructions even rehearse the key connections that must be drawn among story elements in support of a consistent interpretation of the defendant's behavior. For example, the following instructions from an actual robbery trial indicate that the actor and the action must be connected through a consistent set of purposes, agencies, and scenes if a clear meaning for the action is to be established:

To convict the defendant of the crime of robbery as charged in the information, the state must prove to you beyond a reasonable doubt:

[Actor–purpose–act]   1. That said defendant did willfully and unlawfully take from the person of D____ C____ certain personal property, to wit: wallet and money.
2. That the taking was accomplished against the will of D____ C____.

[Actor–agency–act]   3. That said taking was accomplished either:

                        a. by means of force or violence to the person of D＿＿ C＿＿; or

                        b. by putting D＿＿ C＿＿ in fear of injury to his person; and

[Actor–scene–act]   4. That said act or acts occurred on or about October＿＿, 197＿, in＿＿.

As these instructions indicate, the prosecution case must employ the same underlying story strategy in every trial. There are, of course, numerous plot devices through which a structurally complete and internally consistent story can be constructed. Moreover, as explained in Chapter 6, there exists a rich variety of tactical maneuvers through which the prosecution strategy can be executed. However, the basic prosecution case must attempt to represent the defendant's action within a coherent set of scenes, agencies, and purposes as the action develops over time. To satisfy the minimum structural criteria of a story, an actor and an act must be connected over time through scenes, purposes, and agencies: actor–scene–act; actor–purpose–act; actor–agency–act.

Each of the structural triads in a story corresponds to one dimension of legal proof: the first *situates* the actor and action in time and space, the second establishes the actor's *intent*, and the third covers the behavioral mechanics or *execution* of the act. These particular action terms assume, of course, that the evi-

Table 1. Elements of Story Structure Corresponding to the Categories of Legal Judgment in Cases Based on Direct and Circumstantial Evidence

	Categories of legal judgment	
Elements of story structure	Direct evidence	Circumstantial evidence
Actor-scene-act	Situatedness	Opportunity
Actor-purpose-act	Intention	Motivation
Actor-agency-act	Execution	Capability

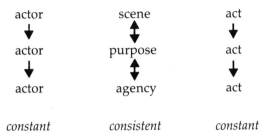

Figure 8. Key Structural Relations in a Credible Story

dence in the case is direct. The prosecution can also establish these factors on the basis of inferences drawn from circumstantial evidence. In cases in which a piece of direct evidence is missing, key structural elements may be inferred from a chain of circumstances. In this case, the components of action translate from situatedness, intent, and execution into *opportunity, motive,* and *capacity.* All of this is to say that the first goal in the prosecution strategy is to define evidence in terms of a complete set of story elements that correspond to the categories of legal judgment shown in Table 1.

It goes without saying that the ways in which actors and acts are defined within any one of the story triads must hold constant across all the structural connections in a story. In other words, the prosecution story must also seek to establish definitions for actors and acts that are constant across the scenes, agencies, and purposes, thereby yielding a consistent and clear interpretation for the actor's act (Figure 8).

The degree to which the prosecution succeeds in fashioning a structurally complete and internally consistent story that takes into account all the evidence in a case determines the probable success of each of the general defense story strategies. A prosecution case that fails to define all of the elements of a story in a consistent way will generally succumb to a defense strategy that simply attacks the structural adequacy of the prosecution case.

A prosecution case that includes a highly selective introduction of evidence (or problematic definitions of evidence) may be vulnerable to a defense strategy that redefines a key element and, thereby, demonstrates the ambiguity of the story. In cases in which the prosecution has failed to incorporate or anticipate a large amount of evidence in its story (or in which definitions of numerous story elements are problematic), the defense may have grounds for constructing a completely new story of its own.

The Defense Strategies

It should not be surprising that the defense's strategic options are more numerous than the prosecution's. Not only does the defense not have to prove the defendant's innocence, but "reasonable doubt" can be created by exploiting different properties of prosecution stories. Most prosecution cases are adequate to the challenge of most defense strategies, but story operations are so powerful that the proper choice of a defense strategy can transform a seemingly airtight prosecution case into a doubtful one. These transformations are often produced without the introduction of new evidence or dramatic eleventh-hour testimony. Storytelling operations make it possible to alter the interpretation of a story's central action through challenge, redefinition, or reconstruction of the story itself.

The *challenge* strategy usually involves some attempt to demonstrate that the key definitions of story elements are poorly supported by evidence or testimony; that the nature of the evidence permits definitions other than the ones the prosecution has assigned to it; or that the prosecution case has some obvious gaps or inconsistencies in it. This strategy seldom requires the defense to put on a case, and it is generally developed through cross-examination and closing statements.

This is an effective strategy when the prosecution does not or cannot present a complete story. Under these circumstances, the defense only needs to review the tacit story model to demonstrate the gaps and ambiguities in the prosecution case. This permits a direct application of basic story tests without committing the defense to redefinitions of its own, which could later come under prosecution attack. A classic case of the effective use of this strategy occurred in the trial of a group of Black Panthers in New York on charges of conspiracy to commit bombings and various other crimes. The prosecution developed its case almost exclusively around the issue of the political motivation of this group to commit the crimes in question. The prosecution was unable to introduce substantial evidence or convincing definitions concerning the capacities of the group to actually carry out the "planned" crimes. (The situational factors were trivial in this case since members of the group met regularly, thereby giving them ample opportunity to plot the alleged crimes.) The prosecution developed clear definitions of motive by demonstrating the admittedly hostile orientation of these "revolutionaries" toward the larger society. Undercover agents introduced a great deal of evidence about the life-styles of these individuals, their speeches about "offing the pigs," and their "plans" to disrupt the lives of affluent white New Yorkers. The motivational elements of the numerous conspiracy stories in this case were established beyond doubt. However, as a result of the prosecution's failure to fill in a complete story around these motives, the defense did not have to redefine elements or construct a new story in order to deal with the definitions of motive established by the prosecution. In fact, the defense was able to accept and even glorify these motives and still win its case. The prosecution evidently discounted the degree to which the jury was bound by its implicit judgment routines. The prosecution seemed to feel that the jury would be swayed by the mere demonstration that these were potentially "dangerous" individuals. As if to remind the jury of its obligation to consider the whole story in judging the defendants, the defense underscored the political beliefs of the defendants, in effect saying, "Sure, we're the worst of the worst, but that isn't sufficient grounds to send us to jail." As Murray Kempton wrote, "Oddly enough, counsel on all sides would begin with the same misconception: Mr. Phillips thought he was prosecuting the armed revolution and his opponents thought they were defending it. Mr. Phillips thought these the worst and Mr. Lefcourt, the best of revolutionaries."[1]

The fact that the defense could zealously agree with the key element in the prosecution case and still win illustrates the power of a missing link in the prosecution story. The state simply did not demonstrate the ability of the defendants to carry out the alleged plots. The impact of the missing element is obvious in the accounts of Kempton, Stephen Chaberski, and Edward Kennebeck (the last two were jurors in the case).[2] They all remark on the impact of the efforts to point out this gap—even though the defense seemed to spend a greater amount of energy working against itself by underscoring the prosecution's characterizations of the defendants' motives. For example, Kennebeck commented on the patent inadequacy of the so-called reconnaissance missions through which the defendants were alleged to have gathered information about the targets for bombings. He also balked at applying the label "revolutionary army" to any group that would dispatch a contingent of members from New York to Baltimore to obtain one gun on the eve of a "major attack." Moreover, the dynamite, chemicals, and other equipment necessary to carry out the major operations in the plan never emerged in the prosecution case. Thus, with respect to some of the conspiracy incidents there existed clear gaps in the stories in the slots where definitions of capability should have been presented. In those instances in which some evidence about capability was introduced, the definitions for these elements simply didn't fit with the definitions for the surrounding elements in the story. For example, how could the jury reconcile such story elements as a "revolutionary army" securing "one gun" to launch a "major attack"?[3] So deficient was the prosecution story about each of the counts against the defendants that the 156 counts of conspiracy yielded 156 acquittals.

The Panther trial is unusual in the sense that cases for which the prosecution cannot construct a complete story seldom come to trial. Since most prosecution stories satisfy the minimum judgment criteria (initial completeness and consistency), the challenge strategy is usually the weakest of the available defense strategies. It is obvious that this strategy has little impact on cases that can stand alone as being complete and internally consistent.

Another weakness of the challenge strategy is that since it relies heavily on challenges introduced by the defense during cross-examination, the prosecution is given ample opportunity to repair its story while it is still presenting its case. This can be done by calling new witnesses, recalling past witnesses, or introducing new evidence to corroborate challenged definitions. A case from our sample of a defendant tried on charges of selling narcotics illustrates this weakness of the challenge strategy. The defendant was arrested for selling hashish to a police informant. However, because of a snafu in police surveillance of the transaction, the officers assigned to the case could not testify that they actually observed the money and the dope change hands. During cross-examination it was revealed that the informant (on whose testimony the connections between actor–purpose and actor–agency depended) had been in trouble with the law on narcotics charges before. Since no one other than the unreliable informant actually *saw* the hash change hands, and since no drugs were found on the defendant at the time of his arrest, the defense argued that the defendant could not be connected clearly to the definitions of agency and purpose necessary to interpret his acts as a crime.

The use of this strategy is generally forestalled by making sure that arresting officers witness the incident, or that civilian witnesses are reliable. Even in this narcotics case, however, the prosecution had the opportunity to repair its story successfully. In subsequent examination the prosecutor established the circumstantial evidence that the defendant met with the informant twice at the scene of the alleged drug sale. On the first occasion the informant was accompanied by an undercover agent, and the defendant refused to sell drugs at the informant's request. However, the defendant arranged another meeting with the informant under the condition that the informant come alone. These established circumstances weighed heavily in favor of circumstantial connections between the defendant and the purpose and agency of selling narcotics. This reestablished a complete and consistent story.

The *redefinition* strategy can be more difficult for the prosecution to counter than the challenge strategy. Its success, however, depends on the defense's ability to find a story element that is ambiguous enough to support another definition and, at the same time, central enough to the story to affect the meaning of the central action. Many redefinition strategies do not succeed either because the redefined element was not ambiguous to begin with or because the redefined element is quite peripheral in the story.

A good example of a redefinition strategy that did not succeed in disrupting connections throughout the story triads was employed in a grand larceny case in our sample. The defendant in this case was seen by a department store employee in a back area of the store in which damaged goods were kept, pending their return to the manufacturer. When the employee asked him what he was doing there, the defendant said that he was looking for a rest room. The employee directed him to one and returned to the main floor. Therefore he did not see what the defendant did when he emerged from the rest room and passed the damaged-merchandise area. A short time later, however, another employee saw the defendant walking through the store carrying two expensive leather bags that the employee had seen in the damaged-merchandise room earlier. He asked the defendant where he got the bags. The defendant asked the employee if he was a cop. The employee called store security, and the defendant was charged with larceny and arrested. One component of the obligatory defense strategy here is obvious in light of the basic prosecution story. The defense showed that the rest room was near the storage room and argued that the defendant's purpose for being in the back area was simply to go to the rest room and not to steal the bags.

Despite the potentially successful redefinition of one structural leg of the prosecution case (the actor–purpose–act triad) the defense was not able to redefine elements in the other triads. In light of this, the web of circumstances in the prosecution story still constrained a more internally consistent interpretation of the defendant's motives.

Only if the defense had redefined a key element that restructured the entire network of connections to the central action would it have been in a solid strategic position. Since the characteristics of the scene and the defendant were fairly clear-cut, the defense tried to redefine the act itself. Rather than accept the inference that the central action involved the defendant leaving the storage room with the two bags (clear proof of larceny), the defendant took the stand and claimed that he brought the bags into the store with him. He set the bags down and went off in search of a rest room. Thus, his appearances both without and with the bags were really part of a larger central action in which the defendant entered the store with the bags, walked through the store without them, and picked them up when he was ready to leave. This redefinition, of course, created more questions than it answered. The new version of the defendant's actions left unanswered the obvious question of how the defendant could have obtained bags just like the ones missing from the storage room if he didn't steal them. Also, would a person carrying two expensive leather bags in a store normally leave them unattended while he went in search of a rest room? And so on.

The point of the example is that the success of any redefinition strategy depends on the choice (and availability) of symbols for key story elements that disrupt the connections across story triads. If redefined symbols do not plausibly displace the connections among most key elements in an otherwise complete and consistent prosecution case, the defense may have to account for the discrepancies raised by its isolated claims. We are reminded here of the classic story of the defendant who was seen entering a house from which the occupants had just driven away. When the police arrived, they found the family silver stacked in the middle of the dining room table. A search of the house resulted in the capture of the intruder as he was stepping out of an upstairs window onto the roof. Rather than acknowledge the acts of entering the house, taking the silver out, and exiting through a window as constituent elements of a single act whose only consistent interpretation is "burglary," the defense chose to treat each component of the action as a discrete act connected to a different purpose. Thus, the defendant entered the house because he was looking for a place to sleep. He took the silver out because it was such a magnificent collection that he couldn't help but admire it more closely. Finally, he went upstairs to find a place to sleep. The bedroom was too stuffy, so he stepped out on the roof for a breath of air, and to his surprise he was surrounded by the police. Such inconsistent definitions are not the stuff of which convincing defenses are made.

When the symbols chosen to replace elements in a prosecution story do not create central ambiguities or disrupt whole chains of connections in the story, the defense has little choice but to attempt to redefine numerous story elements one at a time. As the number of redefinitions increases, the members of the jury will naturally attempt to organize these new claims about the action into a story of their own and compare them systematically to the prosecution case. Most such stories, like the "burglar on the roof" story, are doomed to appear inconsistent in comparison to the prosecution case. Instead of adding redefinitions one by one, the defense can more profitably attempt to construct an alternative story to the prosecution case from the outset.

The *reconstruction* strategy usually involves placing the central action in the context of an entirely new story to show that it merits a different interpretation. A common defense in murder cases, for example, is to show that the defendant acted in self-defense. A plausible story on this theme must reformulate the three triads by showing that the defendant could have been at the scene without intending to kill the victim, that the defendant had no prior reason to kill the victim, and that the means of causing death reflected a spontaneous response to serious provocation. Such connections are usually difficult to establish, and the overall strategy makes the entire range of defense story strategies available to the prosecution in formulating its response. The advantage of this strategy, however, is that it often makes judgment in a case dependent on both the structural adequacy of the original prosecution story and the ability of the prosecution to demonstrate structural problems in the defense case.

The nature of the reconstruction strategy and its implications for a prosecution response are illustrated nicely by the narcotics case discussed in Chapter 3. The case was based on the testimony of an undercover agent, M___, that he had made a deal with the defendant's partner, F___, for thirty jars of amphetamines. (A jar equals approximately 1,000 hits.) When M___ arrived to pick up the drugs, F___ came over and checked to see that he had the money. F___ then left the scene and returned later with K___ (the defendant). F___ got out of the car and said that K___ was leaving to get the drugs. K___ left and came back a few minutes later. When he returned, he picked up F___ a short distance away from the police agent's car in the parking lot where the deal was taking place. They then both drove up to M___'s car. F___ got out and asked K___ to lift up a box in the back seat to show M___. As he did this, M___ and the officers with him got out of the car and arrested both F___ and K___. K___ swore when he realized that he had been caught, and he demanded some identification from the arresting agents.

The defense had a completely different account of K___'s actions. This story centered around a central action having to do with problems that K___ was having with his car and his efforts to fix it. K___ testified that he had spent the entire day having problems with his car and trying to fix it so that he could leave on a vacation. The final episode occurred a few hours before his arrest when the car broke down again on the highway. He hitchhiked from the car to a bar where he knew some people. He tried to get a ride home with someone so that he could get some tools. Finally, F____ appeared at the bar. K____ knew him slightly, and he asked F____ to give him a ride home. F____ agreed to do so. On the way to K____'s house, F____ asked to be let out at a local store. He told K____ to go ahead and take the car to his house, get the tools, and come back and pick him up. When K____ got home he talked to his roommates, and they convinced him that it was too late to fix the car that day. So he left his tools at home and returned the car to F____. When he returned to the store, F____ was waiting. He asked K____ to drive over to a parking space beside a car that turned out to contain the narcotics agents. F____ asked K____ to reach into the back seat and give a box to the person in the car. When he did this he was told that he was under arrest. He said he was so surprised to be surrounded by "a bunch of longhairs carrying guns" that he swore at them and demanded to see proof that they were police officers.

This story takes the central action in the prosecution story (driving up in the car with the dope) and places it as the mere denouement in another story in which "trying to get a ride home" was the central action. By relocating the central action in this way, the defense seemed to offer a plausible alternative interpretation for the alleged criminal act. When the defense tells a story of its own as it did in this case, the prosecution is free to employ either of the other two strategies in response. As it happened, the prosecution redefined the key scenic element of the defense story, and this rendered all the structural triads ambiguous. The defendant had not specified the exact location of the bar where he was "stranded" without a ride home. Under cross-examination he was asked how far the bar was from his house. He admitted that it was only a couple of blocks. The prosecution then asked why he spent the greater part of the afternoon waiting for a ride for just a couple of blocks. If the defendant had defined his purpose in seeking the ride as getting him and his tools to the site of his car, not just taking him home, the story would have been much less vulnerable to this redefinition by the prosecution.

Case Construction and Legal Judgment

These brief examples of the three basic story strategies in trials cover all the major strategies found in the trials in our sample (with the exception of those few cases in which the defense merely "walked through" a jury trial to establish grounds for appeal based on due process violations, inadmissible evidence, etc.). Understanding the strategic constraints available to the prosecution and the strategic options available to the defense provides a basis for explaining systematically most of what goes on in a trial. In most trials the major lines of questioning, the legal moves, and the efforts to establish particular definitions for evidence can be understood in terms of how they fit into the evolving story strategies.

When case strategies are selected with sensitivity to the possibilities for challenge, redefinition, and reconstruction, trials become fascinating dramas in which the same body of evidence may be transformed in radically different ways. A seemingly conclusive prosecution case can be rendered meaningless by the right story operation by the defense. An apparently effective defense response can be turned into support for the prosecution case. The importance of selecting the right story strategy is illustrated by the dramatic defense case in the political trial of Angela Davis.

In her book *Jury Woman* Mary Timothy provides a detailed account of the trial of Angela Davis.[4] Davis was charged with murder, kidnapping, and conspiracy in connection with a shootout and prisoner escape attempt at the Marin County, California courthouse in August 1970. The prosecution claimed that Davis, motivated by her love for prisoner George Jackson, had helped his brother, Jonathan Jackson, plan and carry out the kidnapping and escape attempt which resulted in the death of four people. The crucial link between Davis and the crime was the fact that the guns used in the shootout were bought and registered in her name. Several other connections were also established. For example, the prosecution demonstrated that Davis was in love with George Jackson, and that she was a leader of a political movement working for the release of a group of political prisoners known as the Soledad Brothers, a group in which George Jackson was a key figure. The prosecution also established that Jonathan Jackson and Davis saw one another frequently in the weeks preceding the crime, and that they had the time, motivation, opportunity, and capacity to plan the escape of the Soledad Brothers. The prosecution further tightened this web of circumstance by showing that Davis bought the guns and ammunition just a short time before they were used in the crime. Finally, the state established that Davis had been at the San Francisco airport (not far from the scene of the crime in Marin County) at the time of the incident and that she flew to Los Angeles shortly after the attempt failed. From Los Angeles, she flew to New York City, where she was picked up several months later wearing a disguise and using a false name. The prosecution claimed that Davis waited at the airport for word of success or failure and, hearing about the failure, she implemented a plan to go into hiding.

In light of the definitions attached to the evidence, this is a plausible account. There are no ambiguities among the connections, and there are no gaps in the specification or connection of the key structural elements (scene, act, actor, agency, purpose). In short, the central action (purchasing guns and ammunition) is well constrained in a manner consistent with the legal definition of the crime in question. This sort of case should bode well for a guilty verdict. In fact, when the prosecution rested its case, Mary Timothy acknowledged that it seemed both complete and convincing.

The prosecution's case seemed incredibly complete. As Mr. Harris [the prosecutor] had itemized the events implicating Ms. Davis, one could almost hear the previously open minds of the jurors clicking shut. I firmly believe that if the jury had to make its decision at that precise moment, it would have been twelve to none for conviction. Every one of us would have voted "GUILTY!"[5]

The trial rules, however, require jurors to withhold judgment until all the information is in. This means that the prosecution story must answer both to the criteria of the general story model *and* to any alternative formulations offered by the defense. The defense in the Davis case recognized that the plausibility of the prosecution story depended a great deal on the problematic definition assigned to one key element: the actor. The defense strategy hinged primarily on the successful redefinition of the actor. The first move of the defense in the Davis trial was to expand the definition of the defendant. Whereas she had been described in the prosecution's account as a woman in love, *tout court*, the defense stressed her professional role as a college professor and her political identity as a disciplined political activist committed to nonviolent means of achieving her goals. Her many past successes in freeing prisoners through legal means were offered to support these definitions. This shift in the portrayal of the defendant seems to have had the most profound effect on the plausibility of the prosecutor's account. The defense, however, also introduced alternative definitions for several other major points in the prosecution case. For example, it was suggested that Davis bought the guns and ammunition for her own protection and for the protection of some politically active friends who were too poor to buy their own arms. A quick review of some of her hate mail gave support to the necessity for some form of protection. The defense also pointed out that Davis had not *fled* to Los Angeles—she lived and worked there. She frequently flew between San Francisco and Los Angeles, and her "flight" on the day of the crime could hardly be considered unusual. She admitted that she did flee to New York City and went into hiding there. However, she did this only after she had been named as the prime suspect of the case. When the defense concluded its redefinition strategy there were inconsistencies in each of the triads (actor–agency–act, actor–purpose–act, actor–scene–act), as shown in the diagram in Figure 9.

Several ambiguities were created in the prosecutor's original coherent and complete story. Speaking from a juror's perspective, Mary Timothy found that she could have believed the prosecutor's story in spite of the defense justifications for the purchase of guns and ammunition and its explanation of the flight from San Francisco. She could not, however, accept the gap between Angela Davis, college professor and nonviolent political activist, and the type of person, swept away by passion, that the prosecutor portrayed. In other words, the description of Davis that the defense had succeeded in establishing no longer fit comfortably with the agent described in the prosecutor's case. This disruption in the connections between the agent, the act, and the purpose became a major element of doubt in the deliberations of the jury, and the jurors returned a unanimous verdict of "not guilty."

This case illustrates nicely the power of story structure in judgment. Neither the defense nor the prosecution had a clear edge in terms of superior documentation for its case. The key story elements on which the judgment and comparison of both cases hinged were equally true: that is, Angela Davis was in love with George Jackson, and she was a committed political activist who had demonstrated success with the use of legal means of securing her political goals. Had the defense failed to suggest the latter symbolization of the defendant, there would have been no grounds for reevaluating an otherwise complete and consistent case. Similarly, had the prosecution chosen another definition of Davis and her motives (say, as a political activist who had become frustrated with legal channels) the defense case would have presented a much less compelling contrast. In short, the terms of judgment were established in the story lines of the defense and the prosecution, and the key judgmental issue in the case involved a structural element over which both sides had considerable definitional leeway.

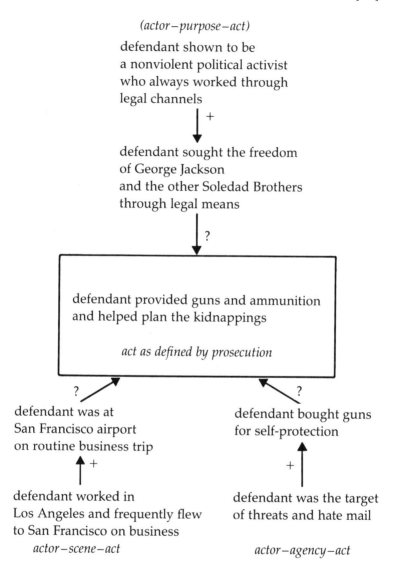

Figure 9. Defense Redefinition Strategy in the Angela Davis Case, Designed to Create Ambiguities in the Story Structure

Not only were the terms of judgment dictated by the story structure (as opposed to the raw evidence, for example), but the judgment process as described by Timothy corresponds to the cognitive operations that we specified in Chapters 3 and 4: the case was quickly reduced to story form; connections were established among key structural elements; and the basic structure of scene, act, agent, agency, and purpose set up implicit tests for consistency, completeness, and comparative plausibility of the connections drawn in the competing accounts. The power of a complete and consistent story to dictate the terms of judgment is illustrated nicely by Timothy's initial reaction to the prosecution case. The characterization of Davis as a radical woman who was passionately in love with George Jackson can be understood in an abstract sense as being normatively and empirically consistent with the actions at the center of the state's criminal case. Most audiences of such a story would be aware of other instances (in fiction or in fact) in which lovers have helped one another escape from prison. Furthermore, the action is consistent with our ideas about love and how people in love ought to act (i.e., they ought to be prepared to come to one another's aid). Thus the connection between the agent (Davis), the purpose (freeing George Jackson), and the act are clearly established through the normative and empirical rules governing our notion of "true love." These connections might even be strengthened through the use of stereotypes about black people or the desperation of separated lovers. When, however, the defense pointed out that Davis was a college professor, known for her nonviolent political activism, who had helped free several black people from prison through legal means, the prosecutor's categorization was no longer a unique definition of the defendant. The structural element "woman motivated by passions" was no longer the only basis for connecting Angela Davis to the central action. Thus, the essential link from agent to purpose, which in this case links the agent to the act, was broken. The structural isolation of competing and equally plausible definitions of key story elements created an ambiguity between the purpose and the act.

In many respects, the situation of a juror presented with such a case to judge is not unlike the position of the audience for the simple stories analyzed in Chapter 4. Neither the juror nor our story audience could question the storytellers directly or ask for clarification of their accounts. They had to be content to judge the stories as they were presented. Unexplained details, gaps in the stories, confusing linkages, and competing definitions for the same structural elements simply remain for the audience to puzzle over. Trial cases and our simple stories are also similar in the fact that the audience members understand that the accounts must be regarded either as true or as probably false, and, in the end, they must commit themselves to either believing or not believing them. These similarities suggest that jurors, like the story audience, must evaluate trial cases according to structural considerations, and that they will pay attention to the same story features for the same reasons.

There are, of course, some obvious differences in the judgment tasks of jurors and our story audiences. The gravity of the courtroom situation and the consequences of the verdict must have some impact on the way jurors listen to cases. We expect, however, that these factors weigh in favor of a more rigorous application of story evaluation routines rather than an increased reliance on such superficial indicators as whether the storyteller had an honest face or a firm voice. (These kinds of considerations occasionally appeared in the explanations offered by our story audiences about the bases of their judgments.) We suspect that in addition to the importance of the judgment, the practice in trials of using multiple tellers to construct a single story also weighs against any systematic reliance on the personal characteristics of the tellers and in favor of the analysis of the structure of the overall story. Another difference in the two experiences is the fact that in trials documentation must be offered in conjunction with the major elements of the stories. This places some limits on the range of plausible stories that can emerge around a given central action.

Despite the greater reliance on documentation in legal cases than in some other story-construction settings, several considerations argue for the dominance of story structure over the facts in legal judgment. First, the story structure is the means of organizing, testing, and placing an interpretation on the facts. Second, as we saw in the Angela Davis trial, equally well documented definitions can be offered by each side for the same structural element in a story. In the end, it is the fit of the symbolized element into the larger structure, and not the pure documentation for the element itself, that dictates final judgment. Third, alternative definitions are available for virtually any fact or bit of evidence. Once again, the key issue is how the chosen definition fits within the competing accounts of the incident. Finally, evidence is most powerful when it is used rhetorically to suggest a missing link in a case or to support a redefinition of a key element in the opposition case. That is, evidence is most often at the service of evolving cases, not the other way around. A final distinction between trial stories and the simple stories from our experiment is, of course, that trial stories are more complex in terms of sheer detail, the multiplicity of narrative styles, and plot development. However, as we suggested in Chapter 3, the analytic power of the underlying story structure is sufficient to reduce virtually any degree of plot complexity or descriptive detail to simple story form. The manipulation of story terms is an activity that is as central and elegant an aspect of everyday communication as the use of deep grammar structure to code and interpret ordinary speech.

Thus the existence of certain notable differences between courtroom stories and those in our experimental analysis does not vitiate the power of the storytelling model. These differences either are made trivial by the power of the story structure itself or have the effect of encouraging audiences to rely more rather than less on structural considerations in judging the plausibility of accounts in trials. In light of these considerations, it seems reasonable to assume that testimony and evidence introduced in trials are reconstructed in story form by jurors and evaluated according to the minimum criteria established in our theory in Chapter 4.

Understanding the strategies of case construction helps to pinpoint the probable "issues" in legal judgment and to determine the possibility of alternative case strategies in trials. Simply describing case strategies does not, however, explain how they are implemented. The minute-by-minute activity in a trial is an often confusing maze of legal and rhetorical tactics intended to advance a developing strategy. In the next chapter we explore the specific symbolic tactics actually deployed to develop the general case construction strategies.

Chapter 6
Rhetorical Tactics
in Case Construction

The execution of strategies, whether on the battlefield or in the courtroom, requires the careful development and use of tactics.[1] The story strategies outlined in Chapter 5 depend on the success of hundreds and perhaps thousands of tactical moves during the course of a trial. For example, the impact of a chosen strategy may depend on how questions are phrased, whether appropriate definitions can be elicited from witnesses, or whether one piece of evidence can be made to appear more significant than another. It is obvious that most of the action in a trial involves the tactical skirmishes between lawyers over the introduction and definition of evidence. It is not obvious, however, how particular tactical moves actually affect the development of a case. In fact, it is easy to be overwhelmed by the drama and rhetoric of trials and to lose sight of the relation between specific rhetorical moves and the development of particular story strategies.

Such is the mystique of lawyers and the court that it is easy to think that every move, nuance, and gesture somehow affect the juror's judgment of the case. This mystique about courtroom tactics is, of course, enhanced by lawyers, as the following remark by Melvin Belli suggests:

Time and again, I have told apprentices in my office that the moment they enter a courtroom they are on stage. What these youthful swains find difficult to realize is that they are on stage whether they are reciting lines or not! I like to refer them to Act I, Scene ii of *Hamlet*—where the stage is filled with motion and oratory. Only one man, of all those in view, is silent and still. That man is Hamlet. The eyes of the audience go directly to him.[2]

It is indeed possible for lawyers and witnesses to captivate the courtroom audience with theatrics. It is, however, equally clear that some theatrical gestures and even some brilliant lines of questioning have little to do with the development of a coherent story strategy. If the action in a trial is to make sense, it must be analyzed in relation to the story strategies underlying the case. When the tactical moves in a trial are examined for their contributions to story strategies, it becomes possible to identify a simple typology of rhetorical tactics in trials. This typology can be used to distinguish between tactical moves that have direct bearing on the stories in a case and those moves, captivating and dramatic though they may be, that have little impact on case construction.

Facts, Rhetoric, and Reality in the Courtroom

Throughout this study we have suggested that facts or evidence occupy an inherently ambiguous position in trials. For example, one observer described the "facts" in car accident cases as "inveterately ambiguous," by pointing out: "The fact that the driver did not see the pedestrian is at once an explanation of the collision in terms of accident rather than recklessness, and also a suggestion that he was not keeping a proper lookout."[3] What makes a particular fact or bit of evidence take on meaning in a case is not its physical form, the credibility of the witness who introduced it, or the corroborating testimony of several witnesses. These things all play important roles when we weigh evidence and assess its reliability, but they do not determine its significance. What makes a fact or piece of evidence meaningful in a particular case is its contextual role in the stories that make up the case.

The relationship of a piece of evidence to a developing story structure is determined by three symbolic operations. First of all, the way a fact becomes part of a story depends on the specific language used by witnesses (and elicited by lawyers) to *define* pieces of evidence. Second, the structural location or placement of a particular piece of evidence in relation to the other elements in the story affects the *connections* that can be made by the interpreter. Finally, the integrity of a story depends on whether key definitions and connections can be *validated* through supporting definitions or whether they can be invalidated by showing that alternative definitions and connections are equally plausible. The acts of defining, connecting, and validating story elements involve different kinds of rhetorical tactics. Each type of tactic can have a different impact on the developing story underlying a case.

Establishing the Key Story Elements: Definitional Tactics

Most of the action in a trial is centered around the efforts of lawyers to elicit particular definitions of evidence from witnesses. The most common tactic employed in defining evidence is for the prosecution to ask questions that require precise and concrete answers. Answers to very specific questions tend to narrow the possible definitions of evidence to just the ones that fit the prosecution story. A convincing specific definition can make it difficult for the defense to redefine the evidence in a manner more consistent with its case strategy. In response to the narrowing tactics of the prosecution, it is common for the defense to try to undermine these specific definitions and broaden the range of possible interpretations to include definitions more consistent with its story strategy.

An interesting example of this pattern occurred in a lengthy exchange between the prosecutor and the defendant in a drunk driving case. The prosecutor sought to establish that the defendant had been drinking beer prior to his arrest for running a red light. Each question asked by the prosecutor was designed to restrict the answer to a narrow numerical estimate of the number of beers consumed. The defendant's responses, in contrast, attempted to return to his lawyer's earlier line of questioning in which the drinking activity was defined in the context of an extended period during which the defendant had several beers in different social settings. The time factor and the multiple social contexts that the defense wanted to include in its definition of the number of beers consumed tended to put the defendant's behavior in a more sympathetic light and raise doubts about the probable effects of the quantity of alcohol consumed. As the following excerpt from this exchange indicates, the prosecutor tried to limit the definition of the drinking behavior to a strict account of the amount consumed:

Prosecution: How much did you have to drink that evening prior to being stopped by these police officers?
(Objection by the defense)
Prosecution: Answer the question, Mr. H____.
Defendant: Well, now, I was working my locker the whole day on Fisherman's Wharf. I have a locker there.
Prosecution: How much did you have to drink?
Defense: May he be permitted to answer the question, be responsive, Your Honor? He started to . . .
The Court: Go ahead. Let him explain.
Defendant: Well, it will have to all come into this now, what I am going to say.
Prosecution: Fine.
Defendant: I left Fisherman's Wharf . . .

This exchange resulted in a definition of the defendant's drinking behavior that clearly was broader than the definition the prosecutor's questions were designed to elicit. It also shows how it is possible for the opposing lawyer to shape a witness's answers even though he may not be conducting the examination. As a result of these defense tactics, the prosecution had to build its case exclusively around the arresting officers' observations about the physical condition of the defendant. The defendant's testimony did not add to the prosecution's case.

A murder trial offers another example of examination tactics designed to narrow the definition of evidence in order to
weaken its fit in the defense case and to make it consistent with
the prosecution's interpretation of the defendant's behavior. The
defendant was charged with the second degree murder (an act
of passion) of a transvestite whom he had met at a bar and taken
to his apartment. The victim was found dead the next morning
in the defendant's apartment. The defendant claimed that he
thought he had picked up an attractive woman, but when they
arrived at his apartment she undressed and proved to be a man.
The defendant asked him to leave, but he refused. When the
defendant insisted that he go, the man attacked him and he
struck the fatal blow in self-defense. As the defense pointed out
in its closing remarks, a self-defense motive warrants an acquittal on a second degree murder charge. The prosecutor clearly
had to redefine the defendant's actions to call the self-defense
motive into doubt and to be consistent with the intention of
murder. In his cross-examination of the defendant, the prosecutor first established that the defendant had been to the tavern
before. He then asked the logical next question: if he had been
there before, he must have known it was a gay bar. An excerpt
from this exchange shows the definitional strategy of the prosecution and the unsuccessful attempts of the defendant to
shade his responses in a direction more consistent with his
defense:

Q: Over the past year . . . do you think that you went to the C____
   Tavern at least one time every weekend?
A: Oh, yes. Well, not every weekend, but I have been in there before.
Q: Would you say once a week?
A: Not always. A lot of weeks I don't play pool. I go to a lot of places. I
   don't have a particular place I go every week.
Q: You are familiar with the C____ Tavern?
A: Yes I have gone there.
Q: You know where it is at?
A: Yes.
Q: You have been in there a lot?
A: I have been in there.

Q: And you know that it is a place where homosexuals gather?

A: Well, they don't have a big sign over the place saying it is for homo-sexuals. That don't make any difference to me. What I wanted to go in there for was to shoot pool . . .

Q: But isn't it a fact that before you ever went in there that you were aware that this was a place where homosexuals went in there dressed up like women? You knew that, isn't that correct?

A: I have been in homosexual places, not only the C ____ Tavern, but quite a few other places across town, but that being a public place, anybody can go in there. You don't have to be a homosexual to go in there.

Q: You just stopped in and had a beer, but you knew that they came in there dressed like women, isn't that a fact? You can answer yes or no.

A: I imagine so, but I didn't know this particular one was.

Despite the defendant's efforts to leave open the possibility that he thought he was picking up a straight woman, not a ho-mosexual male, the prosecutor's questions elicited answers that clearly cast suspicion on the likelihood of this scenario. This, in turn, removed the foundation for the self-defense motive since under this definition the defendant should not have been sur-prised to find that the person he picked up was a man.

Both of these examples illustrate the use of questions de-signed to produce definitions of evidence consistent with the larger underlying story that is being developed in a case. They also demonstrate the interplay of lawyers and witnesses in the struggle to expand or contract the range of definitions appli-cable to key elements in a case. In addition to the construction of questions, the use of objections, and the efforts of witnesses to avoid answering questions directly, definitional tactics may en-tail specific sorts of teamwork between lawyers and their wit-nesses. One form of teamwork typically involves the lawyer carefully leading the witness through the testimony by offering cues about how broadly to answer a question, what to volun-teer, and what to anticipate in the next question. Another form of teamwork involves the rehearsal of testimony to prepare the witness to deliver precise and confident answers to the questions.

On occasion, the teamwork between witness and lawyer becomes a bit overdone. For example, in a larceny case the mother of the defendant was called to testify in her son's behalf. Even though she had been excluded from the court prior to her testimony she clearly recognized the significance of a piece of evidence in the case and answered the lawyer's question about it before it was even asked.

Defense: Now, calling your attention to state's exhibit nineteen, which is a hat, I am going to show you that hat, and ask you if you have ever seen that hat or a hat similar to it before.

Witness: No. My boys would never wear . . .

Prosecution: I will object to that, Your Honor.

The Court: Sustained.

Prosecution: Her answer is not responsive. She is obviously answering some question from in her own mind, not the question asked.

Defense: Mrs. S____, have you ever seen your son with a hat like this one?

Witness: No, sir, I haven't.

Under most circumstances it is possible for a lawyer to exercise tight control over the testimony of a cooperative witness. Such control generally entails cuing the witnesses about correct responses, the desired definition of key facts in a case, and the proper sequence for the introduction of important story elements. This last type of control is illustrated by the careful orchestration of a witness's testimony in the following excerpt from a burglary trial:

Q: Did you have any discussion with Mr. L____ after you arrived?

A: Yes, I did. The tags on the army truck, he had not . . .

Q: Excuse me just a second, M____. Just answer the question. You had a discussion with him?

A: Yes, I did.

Q: Did you discuss the money which he owed you?

A: Yes, I did.

Q: Did you discuss the truck, particularly?

A: Yes, the truck was . . .

Q: With reference to the truck, had the tags on the license plate been altered on it?

It is clear that the lawyer here wanted to introduce information about the truck in a specific form and in a particular sequence. He first alerted the witness to this by interrupting his testimony, calling him by his first name (he had used his last name up to this point), and instructing him to answer the questions in a narrow fashion. This produced a series of yes-no type answers with little embellishment or anticipation of the forthcoming questions. When the witness once again anticipated the answer to the next question, the lawyer simply interrupted him and asked the question that he wanted to introduce next.

A similar tactic was employed by the defense attorney in the examination of his client in the murder trial discussed earlier. The lawyer attempted to establish the precise sequence of action from the time his client picked up the victim in the bar until the time he struck and killed him. Part of the defense case involved the claim that a cabdriver who contributed an important bit of evidence to the prosecution case was not the driver who drove the defendant and the victim home that evening. The defendant was so eager to deliver this bit of information that he attached it as a non sequitur to the end of an answer to another question. The lawyer simply ignored this part of the answer and proceeded to develop the ongoing line of questioning until he reached the appropriate juncture at which to ask the witness to provide the information about the cabdriver once again.

Q: How were you feeling? Were you sober?
A: I was a little bit high. I don't usually get high. I don't drink that much. The cabdriver that was questioned, he wasn't the cabdriver in the first place.
Q: What did you do then?
A: Well, I was standing there and finally decided that she looked pretty good to me.
Q: Now this was on Saturday night?
A: Yes.

Q: And you say that the person that testified that said he was the cabdriver was not the one that drove you that night?
A: Yeah.

It goes without saying that the degree of success in a lawyer's attempt to engineer the course of testimony depends a great deal upon the willingness of the witness to cooperate and his or her ability to respond to the cues in a line of questioning. Some witnesses are more cooperative and more receptive to cues than others. As a rule, expert witnesses (detectives, doctors, criminologists, and the like) called by the prosecution are the most effective partner with whom to play out a tactic of cooperation. Expert witnesses generally have schooled the lawyer in advance on the terminology that can be applied to their evidence. They also tend to be sympathetic to the goals of the state, and they deliver a confident line of testimony. Finally, expert witnesses get a lot of practice in trial situations. This hones their sensitivity to the tactical moves of their examiners. Not only does this experience make expert witnesses excellent players in a cooperation game, it also enables them to disrupt effectively the efforts of opposing lawyers to orchestrate their testimony.

As these examples have implied, the goal of most definitional tactics is to transform bits of evidence into language terms that provide the best fit with one's story about the crime. These tactics may also be directed at upsetting the fit of evidence in the opposition story. Simple definitional tactics are employed when enough of the story structure has been developed to make the location of a bit of evidence obvious, or when the evidence is defined as one of the key structural elements (scene, act, agent, etc.) in the story. In either case, the issues of where the evidence fits into the story is fairly straightforward. Some bits of evidence, however, may not be placed so easily within a story. A definition alone may not be a sufficient basis for interpreting a fact if the surrounding story is too loose or if the same fact occupies different locations in competing defense and prosecution accounts of the alleged criminal activity. Under these circumstances various tactics aimed at establishing connections be-

tween the bit of evidence and other elements in the story may
be employed in addition to basic definitional tactics.

Establishing and Disrupting Connections
in Stories: Inferential Tactics

Most of the examples in the previous section involved central
structural elements whose place in the overall story structure
was clear. In such cases it is usually sufficient to construct (or
disrupt) a definition for these elements in order to make them
interpretable. In other cases, both the definition of an element
and its location in the story may be disputed. When this occurs,
definitional tactics must be accompanied by rhetorical tactics
that show clearly where the bit of evidence fits into the story
and how it is connected to the surrounding action. For example,
suppose that a defendant in a manslaughter trial claimed that
he had checked his hunting rifle before it discharged to kill his
companion, and had found it unloaded. Even if it could be established that he inspected the rifle properly, there might still be
reason to cite him with negligence. For example, if the prosecution could establish that the inspection took place several days
before the hunting trip and that the rifle and ammunition were
available to others during the interim, the defendant could be
expected to have checked the gun again at the start of the trip.
In this case both the definition of the act (i.e., how the gun was
inspected) and its connection to the central action in the case
(i.e., whether the inspection was an event in the distant past or
whether it occurred immediately before the shooting) are required to interpret the significance of the evidence in the story.
As this example indicates, the incorporation of some pieces of
evidence into the overall story strategy requires more than
simple definitional tactics. Various inferential tactics governing
the weight, placement, and connection of evidence in the general story may be employed as well.

The most common inferential tactic involves the struggle over the location of a particular bit of evidence in relation to certain other elements in the story. This tactic often culminates in a blatant innuendo (which is often the object of an objection) about just how the evidence should be connected to the other elements with which it has been placed. For example, both sides in a robbery case agreed that the defendant gave her purse to a companion at some time before a second companion grabbed the victim's wallet and threw it to the defendant, who ran away with it. The defense claimed that the defendant had no prior knowledge that her friend was going to steal the wallet. In fact, the action came as such a surprise that when the stolen object was thrust into her hands she ran away out of fear. In this story there is no connection between handing over the purse and fleeing with the stolen goods. When the defendant was under direct examination, she claimed that she handed the purse to her companion before she even saw the victim. She asked her friend to carry it only because it kept slipping off her shoulder. When the prosecution began its cross-examination, it was clear that its two major objectives were to show that the defendant handed over her purse just prior to the robbery and that she did so to ensure a faster getaway. Although the defendant resisted the prosecutor's attempt to move the action ahead in time, the lawyer was able to make explicit the connection he sought between the act of giving her friend the purse and the defendant's involvement in the crime:

Q: At what point did you give your purse to D ___?
A: Before we got out of the car.
Q: And you testified earlier, I believe, that you gave it to her because you had a leather coat on?
A: Yes. It kept slipping off.
. . . .
Q: You could ball the strap in your hand like a leash, couldn't you?
A: Yes.
Q: Isn't it true, Miss V ___, the reason you gave the purse to D ___ was because you wouldn't be burdened down with it when you ran?

In some cases inferential tactics are less direct than this attempt to state outright the connection that best incorporated the evidence in the prosecutor's strategy. It often happens that a particular connection is established as a result of the presence or absence of other information. For example, the defendant in another robbery case claimed that he ran away from the police at the scene of the crime because in a prior brush with the law he was not given the benefit of seeing a lawyer and was coerced into signing a confession. This inference would disappear quickly if it could be shown that the defendant did have a lawyer in the prior incident, and that he signed the confession on the basis of good legal advice. This is precisely the tactic that the prosecution pursued on cross-examination. As the following excerpt indicates, the lawyer first alerted the jury that he was going to supply some missing information, and then he established the key fact that disrupted the possible inference that the defendant ran from the police because he had good reason to be afraid of them:

Q: Mr. M____, the testimony that you gave yesterday, was that the entire truth?

A: As far as I can recall, it is.

Q: Now, in addition to telling a deliberate falsehood, it is possible also not to accurately convey a situation by omitting details. Did you omit any facts in your testimony yesterday to cast your situation in a more favorable light?

A: I don't think so.

Q: Besides telling a deliberate lie, you can forget to tell something so it was different than it was. Did you forget to tell us anything yesterday to change the facts we talked about?

A: I told it like it happened as far as I can tell you.

Q: Did you review your testimony with your lawyer before you testified?

A: No, not all of it.

. . . .

Q: Yesterday you said you pled guilty to breaking and entering or larceny, is that what you told us yesterday?

A: Yes.

Q: But that doesn't totally convey what actually happened in F ____
County on 14 February, '67 does it?
(Objection which is overruled)
Q: Does it?
A: What was the question again?
. . . .
Q: Now, you told us yesterday at that time you didn't have a lawyer to
represent you, is that right?
A: Well, there was a lawyer there, but he didn't say anything. I done
all of the talking.
Q: So you did have a lawyer then?
A: But he didn't do anything.
Q: Did you talk with him before you entered your plea?
(Objection which is overruled)
Q: Yesterday you said you didn't have a lawyer and today you said
there was a lawyer there now and now I am asking you did you talk
to him before you entered that plea or those pleas?
A: Yes. But he wouldn't give me no advice on what to do. He just said
to do whatever I thought was best.
(Then shows defendant a copy of the guilty plea with both the de-
fendant's and the lawyer's signatures on it.)

In cases in which elements of the immediate story cannot be
manipulated to make or break a particular connection, the next
basic tactic may be to show that a particular inference is in keeping with past behavior of the defendant (or other witnesses) under similar circumstances. For example, if the defendant denies
that his or her behavior carried any knowledge or intent of criminal activity, it is often possible to dispel this inference by showing that on another occasion the defendant behaved in a similar
fashion and was convicted of the same crime for which he is
presently charged. This is a powerful means of establishing inferences about disputed actions in a case. For example, the defendant in the narcotics case discussed in chapters 3 and 5 told a
fairly tight and unshakable story about how he unwittingly
came into possession of the drugs and naively delivered them to
the scene of a sale arranged by the real owner of the drugs. The
defendant presented a fairly convincing picture of an unwitting
dupe who had been tricked into participating in a narcotics

deal. Rather than rearrange the elements in this story directly, the prosecutor merely showed that the defendant had been convicted of the same crime before and that he had used the same defense. This tactic effectively disrupted the defense story and reinforced the inference that the defendant's acts reflected a conscious involvement in the drug sale:

Q: . . . you told us at the beginning of your testimony about the 1973 incident in which you were involved.

A: Yes.

Q: As I understand your explanation, you had no intention of making a drug sale at that time.

A: That's correct.

Q: Kind of you yourself was a victim of circumstances with regard to that earlier conviction?
(Objection which is overruled)

Q: Isn't it a fact that you told the presentence investigator and the judge at your last sentencing that you had nothing to do with the sale and you were the victim of circumstances, that you didn't know a sale was going on?

A: Yes, I believe I said that.

Q: And on that basis they gave you probation; is that right?

A: Yes, sir, they did.

. . . .

Q: Actually this last case involved a sale to an undercover agent, too, didn't it? Isn't that what happened?

A: I assume, yes.

Q: And wasn't it a case where this other guy . . . negotiated the sale and when the sale was negotiated you got the stuff? Isn't that what happened last time?

A: No, it's not, Mr. M____.

. . . .

Q: Isn't it a fact that you then remained present in 1973 when $140 changed hands . . .

A: No, that is not correct, Mr. M____.

In the above line of questioning, the prosecutor established that the actions in the defendant's story represented a direct parallel to a previous criminal conviction in which the defendant told the same story. He then used innuendo to suggest that the defendant's role in the last case was exactly the same as in the present one and that he had lied in his previous defense. This example involves the use of both parallel stories and innuendo to create a clear inference about the disputed actions in the defendant's story. This is probably the dominant tactic employed to shore up cases against repeat offenders.

In most cases in which the inference to be drawn about a clearly defined story element is disputed, the rhetorical tactics center around relocation, innuendo, manipulation (i.e., addition or deletion) of evidence, or the telling of parallel stories. In some cases, however, the evidence introduced by a witness cannot be incorporated in the story strategy by these means. When these standard inferential tactics break down, the dominant rhetorical tendency is to place the evidence in the comparative context of what an ordinary person would do in the situation or what the evidence would mean to an ordinary person. This is often an appealing tactic since it asks jurors to consider what they would have done under the circumstances and what the evidence means to them. Since, however, this tactic involves removing the evidence from a context provided by the witness and placing it in a context tailored to the juror's experiences, it may result in inferences based narrowly on jurors' past experiences. In many cases, what is "ordinary" for the typical lower-class or minority defendant or witness may be quite extraordinary from the perspective of the typical white middle-class juror. For example, larceny cases often center around the issue of how the defendant came into the possession of stolen goods. In many respects, the circumstances surrounding the acquisition of stolen property may be ordinary events in the lives of certain socioeconomic groups and yet seem bizarre or implausible to the average juror. Lawyers often play on this discrepancy in developing a line of questions that challenges the inference that the defendant had no knowledge that the goods were stolen. The following excerpt from the cross-examination of the defendant in a larceny trial set up the inference that the defendant must have known that the merchandise he bought was stolen because he didn't take the precautions that an ordinary person would have taken prior to purchasing the goods:

Q: Did you ask these gentlemen where they had gotten the calculators?
A: Yes.
Q: What did they tell you?
A: They said they bought several of them at a Boeing surplus and these were the last four and they wanted to get rid of them.
Q: Did they show you identification from Boeing?
A: I don't recall asking them for identification.
Q: Did they say they worked with Boeing?
A: No . . .
. . . .
Q: Did you ask them how long they had the calculators?
A: No.
Q: Did you ask them how old the calculators were?
A: No.

The prosecutor went on to ask whether the defendant was aware that he got a particularly good deal on the calculators, whether he was surprised that they were so new, and so forth. The effect of these questions was to support the inference that the defendant should have suspected that the calculators were stolen. In fact, the defendant wrote a check for the merchandise and typed up a bill of sale that both he and the seller signed. Although these do not seem to be the acts of someone who is convinced he is buying stolen goods, these factors were lost in the barrage of prosecution questions about whether he took the precautions that an ordinary person would have taken to make sure the goods weren't stolen.

Both definitional and inferential tactics are aimed at creating the best possible fit between a piece of evidence and the story strategy underlying a case. Although both types of tactics affect the substantive interpretation of a piece of evidence, neither one directly addresses the reliability or credibility of the evidence. Questions of the quality of evidence depend on what might be termed validational tactics.

Establishing the Credibility of Evidence:
Validational Tactics

When definitional and inferential tactics are effective they produce symbolic treatments of evidence that enhance the overall
completeness, consistency, and plausibility of the story in a
case. Even well-defined and connected evidence may, however,
be attacked by special tactics designed to question its validity.
On the other hand, weakly defined and connected evidence can
be strengthened by associating particular treatments of evidence with images of reliability. The primary tactics used to increase or decrease the credibility of particular treatments of evidence are investigating the credibility of a witness and raising
doubts about some part of the testimony.

Lawyers' objections are among the most familiar and over-
used moves in the courtroom. Most objections are designed either to prevent a piece of prejudicial evidence from entering the
record or to build a record of errors in the trial on which an
appeal can be grounded. Many objections, however, are aimed
directly at the jury with the sole purpose of confusing the issue,
disrupting testimony, or introducing reasons why jurors might
wish to discount the evidence in question. Some lawyers rely so
heavily on objection tactics that they raise objections whenever
they hear damaging testimony or need to gather their wits. On
occasion an attorney may object with little apparent reason for
doing so. An illustration of content-free objection carried to absurd extremes is contained in this excerpt from an exchange between the lawyers and the judge following a conference:

Defense: I had an objection, but at this point I can't remember what I
           said earlier was the objection because it's come up so long
           ago. But I am not going to waive my original objection,
           whatever it was.
The Court: Good. Now, with respect to . . .

The most common sort of tactical objection involves objecting
to the admissibility of a clearly admissible piece of evidence in
order to plant concerns in the juror's mind that the evidence

may be suspect in origin, or that the defendant is being rail-
roaded by the prosecution. For example, the law in the jurisdiction from which our sample of cases was drawn clearly permits
a defendant's past criminal record to be entered as evidence
against him if he takes the stand in his own defense. Nevertheless, the clear intent of the law on this point did not keep the
defense attorney in the following excerpt from a murder trial
from objecting "for the record" when the prosecutor attempted
to bring out his client's past record.

Prosecution: Isn't it true that in February of 1964 that you were con-
victed of manslaughter and sentenced to twenty years in
the state penitentiary?
Defendant: Well, yeah.
Defense: We object to that for the record.
The Court: Overruled.

In light of the explicit wording of the law on this point, it is
clear that an objection "for the record" was pointless. Such objections may, however, cause jurors to wonder whether this bit
of evidence is of marginal legality and, therefore, whether it
would be prejudicial to weigh it too heavily. This sort of objection may also be designed to convince a client that his lawyer is
doing everything possible even though the case seems bleak.

Another category of objection functions primarily to disrupt a
line of questioning and to confuse the evidence it was intended
to introduce. For example, the arresting officer in a narcotics
case disrupted the line of defense questioning by claiming that
he did not grasp the point of a rather straightforward question.
Before the witness used this tactic, the prosecutor had made a
series of objections designed to confuse the same issue:

Defense: Detective, . . . do you have an opinion as to whether all of
this paraphernalia would belong to one person or more
than one person?
(Prosecution objects on grounds that this question falls
beyond the detective's area of expertise. Defense points out
that the detective is a narcotics investigator and should
know about these things.)
The Court: . . . Overruled. You may answer, detective.

Witness: Would you repeat the question.
(Defense asks if the quantities of paraphernalia found would ordinarily belong to one person or more than one person. Prosecution objects on another ground and is overruled, whereupon the witness begins to evade the question as noted above.)

Objections are ways of confusing or casting doubt upon evidence that is otherwise clearly defined and reliable. They are probably the most effective tactic to cloud evidence that is defined by competent witnesses who are sure of their testimony. Objections have the potential to affect judgments about evidence and the underlying story structure of the case. For this very reason, however, tactical objections may be weak rhetorical devices. So powerful is the tendency to assimilate a fact that fits well within an emerging story about a case that objections probably damage only evidence that is weak or marginal to begin with. In cases in which a witness is not confident of his or her testimony, or the recollection of an event is hazy, or the witness has reason to lie, a more effective tactic is to challenge the credibility of the witness. An effective demonstration that the witness is either a reliable or an unreliable observer of the incident in question can directly affect jurors' estimates of the validity of the evidence.

The most convincing method of challenging a witness's credibility is to demonstrate that he or she has lied in the course of testimony. Often a witness who is trying either to cooperate or to avoid providing a definition that fits into one of the stories about a case will shade his or her testimony to the point that it may contradict other available facts. For example, the defendant in a robbery case claimed that he wasn't wearing a red T-shirt when he was arrested, and, therefore, he couldn't have committed the robbery since the thief was seen wearing a red shirt. However, in his zeal to demonstrate that he wasn't wearing a red shirt, the defendant made the fatal mistake of claiming that he didn't even own one. The prosecutor seized upon this issue as a means of undermining the defendant's credibility as a witness:

Q: Now, on this evening isn't it a fact that you were wearing . . . a blue jeans jacket and a red tank top?

A: No.

Q: What did you have on?

A: That's not true. I had a white T-shirt like this and a pair of corduroys . . .

Q: No jacket at all?

A: No.

Q: You have got a red tank top don't you?

A: No. Check the files; get the files out there. They got the pictures.

Q: And your testimony is that you have never had a red tank top like the white one you have on now?

A: No. They got the files out there.

Q: I show you part of the files here Mr. H____, exhibit number eight. Is that your picture taken September 3 this year?

A: That is my picture. But when I got arrested, I didn't have this on.

Q: Well, you own a red tank top, though, don't you?

A: I've been arrested prior, but I didn't have that on when I got arrested.

In his concern to demonstrate that he wasn't wearing an outfit similar to the one observed on the thief (a difficult claim to prove), the witness grasped for the most compelling proof by asserting that he didn't own such a shirt. The prosecutor, however, produced a picture of him wearing such a shirt. This blow to the defendant's credibility further undermined his already weak claim that he wasn't wearing a red shirt at the time of the crime. Catching a witness in an outright and self-serving lie is probably the most effective means of invalidating the evidence he or she has contributed to the story underlying a case. However, it is seldom possible to demonstrate that a piece of testimony is a clear lie.

In some cases it is possible to show that a witness has been mistaken about similar things in the past, and that therefore it is possible he is mistaken in the present instance also. For example, the principal witness in a narcotics case was a detective who had been involved in an earlier mistrial because he falsely identified the defendant as the buyer of some drugs. The defense attorney in the subsequent case sought to introduce this misidentification of the defendant into the evidence on the grounds that such a serious error reflected a weakness in the witness's powers of observation. The first attempt to establish the detective's past error failed:

Q: Now, Mr. B____, do you remember testifying in the case of State vs. O____ on February 14, 1973?
Prosecution: Your Honor, I am going to object to this line of questioning. It's not relevant to this case.
The Court: Objection sustained.

Hinting at a grievous error in testimony in a previous similar case was, however, too tempting a move for the defense to pass up. The prosecution closed its redirect examination with a question about how sure the witness was, whereupon the defense opened its recross-examination with a veiled reference to the prior case.

Prosecution: Are you sure of your identification of the defendant?
Witness: Yes.
Prosecution: That is all.

                Recross-Examination

Defense: Are you as sure as you were in the prior case?
Witness: Yes.
Prosecution: Object to that, Your Honor.

This reference was too obscure to convey what had happened in the prior case or what role the detective played in it, but the lawyer's persistent attempts to raise the issue reflect the attractiveness of this tactic as a means of invalidating testimony.

In most cases witnesses do not provide a convenient opening for the lawyer to employ either of the above credibility tactics. If the credibility of a witness is to be damaged in the absence of clear contradictions or past errors, the lawyer must rely on his or her ability either to challenge the witness's powers of recall or to intimidate the witness. Testing the powers of recall of a witness is probably the most pervasive credibility tactic. It does not require catching the witness up in any past or present indiscretion. It depends solely on the lawyer having a greater command of the facts of a case than the witness. It is common for a large portion of any cross-examination to be consumed with dozens of seemingly trivial questions about what happened in the scene that the witness observed. The point of asking a barrage of questions about the fine details of an incident generally is to establish the overall level of certainty against which the principal testimony of a witness can be gauged. For example, it is not uncommon for an individual involved in a crime (particularly the victim or the defendant) to be grilled about the entire day's events, as in this excerpt from a robbery trial:

Q: Now, on this particular [day] do you recall when you got up in the morning?
A: Yes.
Q: What time did you go to work?
A: I went to work at 7:30 in the morning, so I got up about 6:00.
Q: You were up at 6:00 and at work at 7:30?
A: Yes.
Q: What did you have for breakfast?
A: Oh, bacon and eggs.
Q: When did you eat lunch?
A: We eat at 12:00.
Q: What did you eat?

And so on.

In our earlier examples credibility tactics were used during cross-examination to invalidate the testimony of a witness for the opposition. It is also possible to use credibility tactics to enhance the testimony of a supporting witness. For example, it is standard practice to review the credentials of an expert witness in order to substantiate his or her claims about the definition of evidence. A variation of this tactic is common in introducing paid police informants who may be discredited by defense tactics. These witnesses are often portrayed as mercenaries who have grudges against defendants or who are allowed to engage in their own illegal activities in exchange for providing evidence against others. When it is possible to do so, a lawyer will portray a witness who is about to deliver key testimony in the best possible light. This was the case at the outset of the following testimony delivered by an informant in a narcotics case:

Q: . . . you are not a regular police officer, are you?
A: No.
Q: How long have you been working in this capacity?
A: Four years.
Q: How did you get involved in this line of work?
A: I was out with a friend of mine about four years ago, and we were out drinking beer and shooting pool, and he wanted to go see some other people in K____, and we went in the house, and they had a little girl who—this was two days before she was eleven months old. They put some hash in a pipe and showed her how to smoke it, then gave her one tablet of amphetamine—speed—in a glass of chocolate milk to drink it down with. And—I don't know. I just said, "Hey, something is wrong." So I called up King County and talked to Sergeant L____, and he explained the dos and the don'ts and how far I should go.

Given the nature of the various validation tactics, it is easy for them to be carried to extremes. As has been pointed out, the reality constructed through stories in the courtroom is brought in through the eyes of witnesses and redefined through the exchanges between witnesses and lawyers. In other words, the medium through which the aspects of a dispute become "real" for jurors is the language used by witnesses and its fit within the emerging story about a case. It is easy for lawyers to push credibility tactics to the point of absurdity by demanding that a witness prove that what he or she recalled or remembered seeing was, in fact, what took place in the actual situation. This runs against the grain of both the symbolic nature of social reality and the symbolic constructionist principles of justice.

Even though we use language to deliver our accounts of the real world, language usage alone can neither validate nor invalidate those accounts. Validation depends ultimately upon the general frameworks of knowledge that operate in a situation to organize the symbols assigned to "real" phenomena into familiar patterns of occurrence. Examples of these frameworks include the methods and theories of science, the ideologies of religion and politics, and the stories used in adjudication. The definitions in a witness's testimony can be tested to a certain degree and his credibility or the reliability of his memory can be challenged, but ultimately the testimony that he delivers must be accepted on its own terms and judged within the larger frame of the story underlying the case. To continue to demand pure linguistic proof for knowledge that is taken for granted only demonstrates the gap between the world we observe and the language we use to describe our observations. We cannot prove that our verbal descriptions do, in fact, represent any objective reality. We can only assess the degree to which our language usage conforms to the rules and patterns assigned to the real world by general interpretive frames like stories. Thus, when a lawyer pushes a witness to prove, in effect, that he really saw what he claims to have seen, the line of questioning quickly becomes absurd. In short, even though we are sensitive to such above-mentioned *indicators* of credibility as lying, previous error, and bad memory, we cannot demonstrate inaccuracy in a naive and seemingly honest observation except by considering how the observation fits into the larger story about the incident.

Attempts by lawyers to discredit witnesses by having them prove how they know what they know generally result in absurdity, impasse, and failure. For example, an arson case in our sample contains almost ten pages of testimony in which the victim is asked by the defense attorney to prove how she knows that a picture of her firebombed apartment that the state wanted to introduce into evidence is, in fact, a picture of her apartment. Of course, she was unable to prove this, and the defense objected to the admission of the evidence on the grounds that it hadn't been identified properly. An excerpt from this exchange illustrates the absurd situation that quickly results when the foundations of language and knowledge are challenged directly:

Q: I believe that you testified that this is a picture taken under your window. Is there anything about the picture by which you can positively identify your window?
A: This is the window up here.
Q: How do you know? How do you know it is your window?
A: Well, I observed from the picture.
A: Is there anything about this picture by which you can positively identify your window or your apartment?

After several minutes of this circular line of questioning, the prosecution resumed its direct examination and asked, "Does that look like your apartment window?" When the defendant said "yes," the judge admitted the photograph into evidence on the "weight" of her testimony. Following this exchange a photograph of another window in the victim's apartment was submitted for an evidentiary ruling. This produced an even more absurd line of questioning by the defense:

Q: Is there anything peculiar about this picture that you can positively identify this as being a picture of your apartment?
A: Well, I keep my window like that all the time.
Q: Would you concede there may be other people that keep their windows . . .
A: No. They generally have it open or closed. Mine stays with a crack like that all the time.
. . . .
Q: Is there anything about the window or anything else that you can positively identify as being a picture of your apartment?
A: Well, I know that it's my window, that window cracked like that. I know those are my curtains was up that particular night.
A: You concede other women may have similar curtains?
A: No one else have curtains like that in the neighborhood.
Q: Do you know in what neighborhood this picture was taken?
. . . .
Defense: I object to state's no. 2 on the same grounds, not positively identified.
               Direct examination continued
Prosecution: . . . Does that look like your kitchen window?
Witness: Yes.
Prosecution: And does that look like your apartment building?
Witness: Yes.
Prosecution: We offer state's exhibit no. 2.

Defense: Same objection.
The Court: It will be admitted.

This is by no means an isolated case of a validation tactic taken to extremes. In a murder trial a witness was subjected to a similar line of questioning to establish how she knew that a distinctive coat offered in evidence was the same one worn by the defendant on the night of the murder. The example of an arresting officer in a narcotics case being asked how he knew for sure that the car that drove up alongside him had its engine running has already been discussed. In a larceny case a witness was repeatedly asked how she could be sure that the branches of a nearby tree did not obstruct her vision, to which she could only reply, "They weren't in the way, because I couldn't have seen [the defendant] if they were in the way."

Conclusion

The effect of carrying validation tactics to their absurd extremes suggests several important things about rhetorical tactics in the courtroom and the underlying nature of justice. First, as suggested earlier, virtually all of the surface rhetorical tactics that are synonymous with courtroom action are tied to an underlying story frame that guides their interpretation and, thereby, determines their impact. If this were not the case, validation tactics aimed at demanding direct linguistic proof for observations would not be so frustrating for witnesses, so pointless to observers, or so ineffective in altering the status of evidence or testimony.

In short, the factor that determines the impact of various rhetorical tactics is their relationship to the underlying story structure. Whether or not it is clear what a lawyer is trying to do with a line of questioning depends on the construction of a story frame in which the responses to the questions have a place. Whether or not a particular definition of evidence or the alteration of connections among story elements produces a significant impact on judgment depends on the centrality of the definition in the story structure or the consistency of the new connections with the larger pattern of connections established in the story. When surface rhetorical tactics lose touch with the underlying story (as in the example in which the witness's testimony was isolated from the surrounding story context and subjected to impossible standards of proof), they lose their effectiveness.

This does not imply that mere references to the surrounding story in a case is sufficient for a particular rhetorical tactic to sway the judgments of jurors. This is a necessary but not a sufficient condition for rhetorical usage to have an impact on the outcome of justice. Once a bit of evidence has been transformed into a story element, the basic stories in a case are still judged both in comparative terms and with absolute considerations about consistency, completeness, and plausibility. Thus, the minimum criterion for judging a rhetorical move in a trial is whether it establishes some fit between a piece of evidence and the evolving story strategy in a case. We can, however, specify more detailed criteria for evaluating courtroom rhetoric. For example, *definitional* tactics tend to be effective according to the extent that their targets are central elements in the story and in proportion to the degree that they move a story toward a completed structure. Antagonistic definitional tactics tend to be effective to the extent that they undermine central elements or create gaps within the story structure. *Inferential* tactics are effective when they establish a network of connections that clarifies the significance of disputed or problematic story elements (usually the motive or the identity of the actor who committed the alleged criminal act). Inferential tactics operate under the constraint that they must clarify the meaning of key story elements and at the same time remain consistent with the larger set of connections established by the ongoing story about the case. *Validational* tactics are effective when they take a piece of evidence, the definition or location of which enhances a particular story, and demonstrate that there are grounds elsewhere in the story or in the behavior of the witness to validate or invalidate the evidence.

Analyzing courtroom tactics in this way allows us to view the maze of trial rhetoric (the varieties of objections, the profusion of examination styles, the haggling over terms, etc.) within a coherent and logical framework. This guards against the tempting mistake of viewing rhetorical moves as self-contained events that can be evaluated in terms of their intrinsic drama, their immediate impact, or their demonstrable success in creating the impression desired by the speaker. The story perspective makes us sensitive to the fact that it is possible to make a dazzling move that has little to do with the key judgmental issues in a case. Moreover, it is possible to establish a clear definition for a bit of evidence that has only a distant connection to the central action in a story or that later becomes difficult to integrate into the network of connections necessary to incorporate subsequent evidence into the story. In short, it is not possible merely to add up some "rhetorical score" to assess the impact of rhetorical tactics on the outcome of a case. An otherwise brilliant case may be lost because of the inability to establish a key definition, make a crucial connection, or fail to undermine an important link in the opposition case.

In addition to providing concrete standards for judging the impact of courtroom rhetoric, this perspective illustrates graphically the fluid symbolic terms through which justice is produced. Trial justice consists of one symbolic universe (that of language and rhetoric) laid upon another (that of symbolic representations of action in story form). The physical or "object" world enters the production of justice only at several steps removed from the terms on which judgments are ultimately based. In this fluid symbol system the real world and the symbolic representation of it in the courtroom are in tension. On the one hand, courtroom stories must be built on definitions of the material evidence that comes from the incident in question. In this sense "the facts" do exercise some constraint over the possible stories that can emerge in a case. However, this constraint is considerably less binding than the conventional mythology of justice shared by most legal professionals and ordinary citizens would indicate. Each fact introduced in evidence is subject to a whole range of definition and placement tactics, the selection of which affects the contextual relations between the fact and all the other evidence that has been defined in story form. Each fact in a case, then, is subject to the permutation of meanings determined by its possible definitions, its possible connection to other story elements, and the variety of meaning that comes from altering definition and connection in relation to all the other definitions and connections in the ongoing story. In the final analysis, it is less the role played by evidence in the natural event than the degree to which the evidence can be redefined and relocated within stories and about the event that determines the outcome of a case.

All of this suggests that it may be misguided to look to such factors as the social biases of jurors, the dispositions of judges, the socioeconomic backgrounds of defendants as key variables in justice processes. All of these factors may seem to play a role in criminal justice and judgment, but their true role is most likely manifested in the discrepancies in language skills, patterns of language usage, and cognitive styles characteristic of different groups in society. In light of this analysis it is reasonable to propose that the key variables in justice processes involve facility with language, the ability to manipulate concrete facts within abstract categories, and the manner in which interpretive contexts that represent social reality are structured. In their most basic forms such objects of contemporary concern in the justice system as bias, social prejudice, inequality of representation, and conflicting values are, like justice itself, functions of how people define the worlds they live in and whether the symbolic structures through which they represent those worlds are shared with others.

PART IV
IMPLICATIONS FOR A THEORY
OF TRIAL JUSTICE

Chapter 7
Toward a Theory
of the Criminal Trial

The collection of variables that has been mobilized to study the trial in the current literature has little theoretical coherence. This results largely from the failure to identify the broad social organizing principles like story construction that underlie the trial and the resulting tendency to break the trial into its isolated commonsense components for purposes of study. The literature on trials is fragmented into topics that correspond to the obvious everyday characteristics of trials: lawyers and their behavior, jurors' dispositions about the case and their attitudes to authority, the characteristics of defendants and their crimes, judges' behavior and their instructions to the jury, and the formal rules of the court. These research areas represent the most obvious properties of trials from a casual observer's standpoint. However, the lack of perspective on how they fit into the more general scheme of justice makes it difficult to explain why these things may affect the judgment about a case. There is even less discussion in the literature about when these various factors can be expected to enter into judgments about a case. Any model of the trial that incorporates only the formal and obvious aspects of the courtroom situation will miss the most important and subtle aspect of the social organization of justice: the way in which formal social procedures unite general principles of justice with the underlying cognitive operations that both embody them and bring them to bear on unique cases. Thus, organizing a model of the trial around the relevant social and psychological storytelling concepts enables us to explain the outcomes of justice in terms of the specific symbolic processes that produce them. This not only tells us how ordinary people "do justice," but helps to explain systematically the importance of the whole array of minor variables (type of crime, defendant characterisics, juror characteristics, etc.) that can have clear but unpredictable impacts on trial verdicts.

It is clear that seemingly extraneous factors, such as the race of the defendant or the nature of the crime, can affect verdicts and sentences. It is not clear, however, how these factors enter jurors' judgments or how they fit into the larger scheme of evidence around which the judgment process is focused. The story construction perspective offers a straightforward explanation of how evidence is integrated with various extraneous factors in the judgment process: some stories are structured in ways that make the information related to variables like defendant characteristics, lawyers' maneuvers, or variations in judges' instructions more relevant for judgment. When a particular story makes it possible for key inferences to be based upon information introduced through a legal maneuver like an objection or a social bias about a type of defendant, such information has a greater probability of entering the judgment process. In other words, stories serve a screening function. The evidence introduced into a trial through legal procedures is at the center of the story construction task. However, particular story structure may make it possible for inferences to be influenced by a variety of understandings about factors ranging from the categorical interpretation of the judge's instructions to stereotypes about the behavior of particular social groups.

The idea that stories serve as screening mechanisms for extraneous influences on legal judgment clarifies some questions about bias in the justice process. For example, the use of stories in legal judgments explains why extraneous factors do not always enter the judgment process. Even though jurors may in some cases be prejudiced against defendants, the stories that best encompass the evidence may not make information about the defendant's race or social status relevant for interpretation.

Similarly, lawyers may make many dramatic moves during a trial, but these moves may or may not affect the interpretation of key ambiguous elements in stories. In other words, the story model explains when extraneous variables are likely to enter the legal judgment process and how these variables become integrated with the bodies of evidence that are supposed to constrain judgments.

The story construction perspective casts a different light on the importance of factors like jurors' social prejudices and lawyers' dramatic maneuvers. Such factors become relevant in trials only when they intersect with central judgmental issues in stories. This explains why statistical associations between extraneous factors and trial outcomes tend to be sporadic. Furthermore, the story model suggests that the best way in which to minimize the effects of extraneous factors in trials does not necessarily involve removing all such factors from the courtroom. It is inconceivable that social prejudices can be wiped out of jurors' minds, and it is equally unlikely that all lawyers can be induced to behave in precisely the same ways during the course of a trial. But if we can identify the cognitive-communicational structure of legal judgment, then it should be possible to detect story strategies that make extraneous factors more or less likely to enter judgments. If such story characteristics can be monitored, then it should be possible to make formal rulings about the acceptability of cases and to alert participants to the likelihood that particular factors will enter judgment in a particular case.

Perhaps the most important payoff of the story construction perspective from a theoretical standpoint is that it makes it possible to reinterpret a large body of traditional thinking about the effects of various factors on legal judgment. Instead of viewing the trial as a black box in which any number of separate factors operate in mysterious ways, the story perspective shows how those factors enter the judgment process and how they can operate together to affect trial outcomes. The following discussions of lawyers' maneuvers, jury characteristics, and aspects of cases and defendants show how conventional topics in the literature can be reinterpreted and integrated theoretically in light of the story construction model.

The Maneuvers of Lawyers in the Courtroom

From the detached observer's standpoint, the lawyers appear to be the dominant forces in a trial. They construct and present the cases. They call witnesses, establish a line of questioning, raise legal points, and school the jury in the subtleties of a case. The trial seems to be their show. They orchestrate the performances and sustain whatever dramatic punch a trial may have. It is tempting to attribute some considerable portion of a trial outcome to their respective displays of style, charisma, body language, witness sequencing, rhetorical strategies, and diversionary legal maneuvers. Analyses of such aspects of lawyers' behavior abound in the literature, but they add up to very little in the way of satisfying explanations of trial dynamics or outcomes. This is not because lawyers are unimportant, but because it is a mistake to carve out the lawyer as a unit of analysis. The analytical decision to isolate the surface behavior of lawyers from the surrounding context of the trial removes this behavior from the underlying dynamic of the setting that makes it a central or peripheral factor in the juror's perception of a case. As shown in Chapter 6, if rhetoric, style, legal moves, diversionary behaviors, and the like, matter, their impact lies in their connections to key structural elements of the stories in a case. In other words, it is simplistic to explain the effectiveness of lawyers in narrow terms of oratory, charismatic presence, or legal knowledge. Effectiveness is more a function of whether these and other resources can be employed selectively at critical junctures in the development of the overall story about a crime.

Since a narrow focus on lawyers detaches them from the story context that makes their contributions to a trial obvious, the resulting explanations of lawyers' behavior seem vague and unconvincing. For example, in Wellman's classic on the skills of cross-examination we are told:

There is no short cut, no royal road to proficiency, in the art of advocacy. It is experience, and one might almost say experience alone that brings success. . . . The experienced advocate can look back on those less advanced in years or experience and rest content in the thought that they are just so many cases behind him. . . .

[The art of cross examination] requires the greatest ingenuity; a habit of logical thought; clearness of perception in general; infinite patience and self control; power to read men's minds intuitively, to judge their characters by their faces, to appreciate their motives; ability to act with force and passion; a masterful knowledge of the subject matter; an extreme caution; and, above all, *the instinct to discover the weak point* in the witness under examination.[1]

By way of illustrating these almost mystical qualities, Wellman reports the following gaffe that occurred during cross-examination in a case contesting a will. The person being examined was a legal secretary who had witnessed the signing of the will. She testified under direct examination that the testator appeared sane at the time he signed the will. At the outset of the cross-examination the plaintiff's counsel initiated the following unfortunate line of questioning:

Q: Have you ever in your life seen anyone who it was claimed was insane?
A: (witness pauses, giggles) I guess I have—I have been employed in an insane asylum for the last two years as an attendant.[2]

The moral of the example, of course, is that the "good" lawyer would never have posed such a risky question to a witness whose background had not been looked into carefully. Similar examples appear in other representative works on the courtroom arts of lawyers.[3]

It is not surprising that such analyses are not far removed from the sort of commentary on lawyers one encounters in the news media and in such popular culture outlets as crime novels, television series, and films. The reason for this similarity is simple. If one views lawyers independently of the underlying dynamics of trials (as any observer of a trial is tempted to do), the overwhelming impression is that some ineffable psychic qualities must determine their impact on a case. A good example of this impact of observational frame on the perceptions of trial observers is found in the extensive national press coverage of the 1976 trial of Patricia Hearst for armed robbery. For example, we were told by *Time* that the trial hinged on a "duel" between the two lawyers. Given the popular stereotypes about what lawyers bring to a case, it was not difficult to detect *Time*'s anticipation of the outcome of the trial. Referring to the two lawyers, *Time* described the case as a duel that

was a dramatic contest for both. A conscientious but colorless prosecutor, Browning had been overshadowed throughout the trial by defense attorney F. Lee Bailey. Browning had not tried a case in six years. . . . San Francisco lawyers tended to dismiss him with faint praise. . . . But the prosecutor was stubbornly confident he would win: he had the facts, he liked to say. Bailey himself posed the problem that would face Browning when he began the cross-examination that lasted two days. If Browning pressed Patty too hard, thus making her a sympathetic figure, warned Bailey, "he will be cutting his own throat."[4]

Newsweek developed the duel theme into the following mixed metaphor:

Bailey's duel with prosecutor James Browning was disappointingly one-sided. Like Muhammed Ali sparring against the amateur champion of Lichtenstein, Bailey alternately feinted and bombarded his victim, luring Browning into embarrassing traps and watching his discomfort with unveiled contempt. On occasion, he even predicted the round in which he would score his daily knockout: after purposely avoiding any direct examination about Patty's alleged love for slain SLA member William Wolfe, Bailey told a cocktail hour staff meeting: "Browning won't be able to resist the subject tomorrow. And when he gets to it, he'll get quite a surprise." Browning didn't resist—and plodded head on into Patty's show-stopping punch line, "I couldn't stand him."[5]

Coverage of the trial consistently homed in on the sort of gaffe that Wellman and others cite to distinguish good lawyers from bad. For example, much was made of a prosecution bumble that introduced a line of testimony that the defense had been specifically prohibited from bringing out in its case. Recall that Ms. Hearst had been kidnapped by the political group with whom she later robbed the bank. Bailey tried to establish that she had been forced to participate in the robbery in response to threats made by the group to bomb her family's estate (San Simeon) south of San Francisco. The judge refused to admit this line of questioning. The next day, however, the prosecutor introduced this testimony inadvertently when he asked the defendant why she felt unable to escape her abductors. She reiterated the threats that had been made on her person, and then made a vague reference to the threat that had been carried out against her family—a bit of information that had been withheld from the jury by the prosecutor's own objection:

"It's happening like that now on the streets," Patty said in a vague way that should have been a warning signal to the prosecutor. Puzzled, Browning said: "What do you mean, Miss Hearst?"

"He's asked the question," cried Bailey, leaping to his feet as Browning tried to change it.

"Well, just a moment, I'm not going to let you tailor her answer," Judge Carter admonished the fumbling prosecutor.

"I may not withdraw the question?" Browning asked quickly, but the judge shook his head.

"Well, San Simeon was bombed," said Patty, eyeing Browning in triumph. "My parents received a letter threatening their lives if I took the witness stand."[6]

The point of all this, of course, is that the defense attorney here may have outwitted, outsparred, and even "outgladiated" (another popular image in the trial coverage) his opponent, but he still lost the case. This was in spite of the fact that many jurors were admittedly sympathetic to the defendant and expressed regrets that they had not heard a convincing refutation of the prosecution case. If we expand on the analysis presented in Chapter 3, we can only conclude that both the brilliance of the defense lawyer and the ineptitude of the prosecutor were misplaced in the context of the structure of the basic stories in the case. The prosecution established a consistent interpretation for the defendant's actions by showing that she had every opportunity to escape from her captors if she had had the conscious desire to do so, and the defense failed to address the one possible explanation for these apparent mental lapses (or, as the prosecution argued, displays of willing compliance): brainwashing. Thus, the skills of lawyers can be explained systematically only as they relate to the definition or emphasis of key elements in a story, not as they bombard the observer with perceptions of dramatic moments or dazzling moves in the course of a trial.

The Jury

For the most part the jury, too, has been approached as an isolated unit of analysis and described in terms of standard commonsense demographic and group dynamics concepts. As we suggested in the case of lawyers, if an object of study is split off from its natural context, there remains little choice but to view it in terms of its most obvious generic properties. Thus, many jury studies persist in analyzing such properties of juries as the jurors' age, sex, income, race, religion, occupation, and education. These demographic characteristics have been supplemented in other studies by such group dynamics concepts as the size of the jury, the role of the group leader (foreman), the method of deliberation, the means of selecting a leader, the degree of mutual censorship or encouragement to air doubts, and the method of registering preliminary verdicts.

The results of the group dynamics studies have been less than conclusive. Some of these inconclusive results have nevertheless been regarded as significant. For example, several studies of the effect of jury size on the dynamics and outcomes of deliberations have yielded no clear patterns.[7] Yet on the basis of these findings, some court systems are experimenting with smaller juries in some types of cases. While most of these experiments in court reform seem benign, there is some cause to worry that they are based on little theoretical understanding of the connections between case structure and deliberation patterns. Studies of jury demographics have turned up a few more conclusive results, but they display a similar absence of theoretical insight. For example, the classic piece of research in this area showed that high-status persons were most likely to be chosen as foreman.[8] They were also more likely to participate actively in deliberations. Higher participation, in turn, was associated with greater satisfaction with the verdict. The general conclusion from this research was that men and high-status people have more influence and derive more satisfaction from jury duty. Strodtbeck pursues some of the implications of these findings in later discussions, but he offers little insight about how they figure in any general scheme of justice in American criminal trials.[9]

Despite their dubious theoretical significance, findings about such variables as the social status of jurors seem to many analysts to be important. Part of their appeal probably lies in their apparent consistency with other research on group behavior. They even echo findings from other fields. For example, political scientists have shown that high-status people (and men more than women) tend to participate more in politics and to feel more effective politically as a result. In courtroom research, however, what effect these patterns have on the scope and bias of justice remains an unanswered question. Do higher-status persons bring different understandings to bear in deliberations? If so, when, and with what effect? In their judgments do they structure their images of the "normal" social world differently from other sorts of people? In recent years, there has been increased concern about these sorts of questions. Jury studies are turning increasingly to the investigation of the cognitive skills and personal dispositions that figure directly in a juror's thinking about a case. These approaches seem to hold out the promise of much better understanding about what it is that jurors bring to a case than the comparatively crude demographic approaches that leave us guessing about what variables like sex, age, or income "stand for" in the trial context.

Most of the work in this area has been done on such cognitive processes and personality-related characteristics as authoritarianism, power motivation, Machiavellianism, internal-external (locus of) personal control, and moral development. The assumption common to these studies is that jurors with certain dispositions may harbor extreme biases that favor one side of a case. These biases may be especially strong in certain types of cases. For example, jurors who score high on measures of authoritarianism and external control may align themselves with the side of the state in "political crimes" (inciting to riot, conspiracy, treason) because such crimes are viewed by the individual as threats to the very basis of social order. Perhaps more important, such individuals may be inclined to accept the state's version of a case merely because the state is assumed to have greater powers of judgment in matters of the law. Likewise, an authoritarian personality might be expected to respond harshly to such crimes as sex offenses, delinquency, and drug abuse—particularly if the defendant displays any trappings of deviance—since these offenses are likely to be seen as direct threats to society and signs of human weakness and moral decay. In a similar vein, jurors at high levels of "moral development" might be more favorably disposed to the defense in certain political cases (e.g., the publication of classified government documents) in which the defense argument rests on the premise that under certain circumstances higher moral public obligations should take precedence over more restricted legal codes. Jurors at lower stages of moral development might be reluctant to see any circumstances that would permit violation of the law, or (at the lowest stages of moral development) they might be inclined to advocate harsh punishment for defendants merely because the state branded their actions as wrong.

It is not surprising that most of the work in this area has been done in conjunction with political trials. Not only do these issues and the dramatization of roles in political trials focus these juror dispositions most clearly, but many of the researchers in this area are concerned with the practical application of their theories to protect the due process rights of defendants whose crimes may arouse certain social prejudices. Among the trials that have become test cases for hypotheses about the social dispositions of jurors and the outcomes of justice are the Chicago Seven, the New York Nineteen, the trial at Wounded Knee, the Joan Little case, the trial of Stephen Solias in San Francisco, the Catonsville Nine and Harrisburg conspiracy cases involving the Berrigan brothers, the trial of Angela Davis, and the New Haven Seven case involving Bobby Seale.[10]

This line of research fits nicely into the development of our general perspective. Political trials illustrate the various aspects of judgment surrounding the storytelling process so well because they often raise issues that strain the underlying principles of judgment on which justice depends. From our standpoint, there are three notable features of a political trial. First, political acts, by definition, reflect serious divisions in public values and norms. As a result, political trials may involve a much wider division in the normative understandings jurors use to interpret stories than most trials do. In a political trial, these disputed normative rules may be central to the interpretation of the alleged criminal action. Second, political trials are more likely than most trials to bring in contact defendants and jurors who live in substantially different worlds. This may not only affect the degree to which defendants and jurors share normative, linguistic, empirical, logical, and aesthetic understandings, but it may affect the ways in which they structure and evaluate stories about social actions. Finally, the legal categories that apply to political cases are often vague (as in the federal conspiracy statutes). This permits a greater range of interpretive license than might be possible in more conventional criminal cases. This, of course, magnifies the potential impact of differences that may exist in jurors' basic understandings or structuring routines.

The implication here is that political trials simply focus and magnify the conditions that can lead to disruptions in the underlying bases of justice in any adjudication. If this is the case, various factors that routinely affect the scope and bias of justice in political trials should emerge (albeit with less regularity and intensity) in other types of cases. For example, we would expect certain kinds of "deviant" crimes to trigger diverse normative and empirical understandings. Defendants and witnesses who come from a variety of encapsulated subcultures (ethnic groups, sexual and political minorities, etc.) may structure their communications differently as a result of different cognitive codings that reflect more accurately their own language conventions, life-styles, and perceptions of ordinary reality.

In this sense, the preliminary findings concerning the psychological dispositions of jurors in political trials can be viewed as special instances of the general interpretative strategies on which jurors rely in any case. The importance of the work on political trials is that it alerts us to the conditions under which differences in basic judgment routines are likely to come into play in all adjudication processes. This should make it easier to locate pathologies of justice in more conventional cases in which these basic conditions are perhaps less numerous or less pronounced. It may also give us a better understanding of what kinds of trials are most likely to engage universally shared understandings and operations at all stages of the storytelling-judgment process. These lessons from the study of political trials and their implications for the storytelling model are ripe for application to a whole range of case and defendant-related factors.

Characteristics of Cases and Defendants

As was the tendency in the analysis of lawyers and juries, most of the early research on the impact of case and defendant traits split off these factors from any larger picture of the trial. The result has been a huge collection of findings showing that most commonsense variables have small effects on trial outcomes.

The most ambitious research on the inventory of case-related factors that affect jury verdicts is reported in Kalven and Zeisel's *The American Jury*.[11] This is a seminal work from the landmark Chicago Jury Project which counted among its data detailed documentation (including survey questionnaires from the judges and members of the jury) on 3,576 cases. The key contribution of this study centered around an attempt to offer a systematic explanation for the verdicts in those 24.6 percent of the criminal cases in the sample on which the judge and jury disagreed about the correct verdict.

Characteristics of the defendant seemed to account for some of these disagreements. In about 4 percent of the cases the jury apparently took the personal qualities of the defendant into account in reaching a decision. More often than not, this worked in the direction of acquitting a sympathetic person (crippled, sick, young, mother, widow, veteran) rather than in that of convicting an unsympathetic person (unattractive, delinquent, single, no family or community ties). There was also a slight tendency toward acquittal in cases in which the crime was seen to have had a strong negative backlash on the defendant already (disruption of family life, loss of job, pretrial imprisonment, damage to reputation, etc.).

In another small percentage of the trials, features of the case or the crime itself were found to account for aberrant verdicts. At times jurors felt that the decision to prosecute a particular case or a particular defendant violated the principle of blind justice. In some of these instances the juror felt that he or she could easily have been arrested for the same "crime" for which the defendant stood trial.[12] At other times, juror perceptions of the law entered the judgmental picture. Some jurors, for example, saw the law as unfair. In these instances the defendant was seen as a hapless victim of justice, not a criminal brought to the bar. In other circumstances, a jury voted to acquit because the possible punishment upon conviction seemed too severe for the crime. This perception may have interacted, of course, with the feeling that the defendant had suffered enough or that a defendant of a certain type (young person, family man, etc.) deserved protection from the ruinous punishment associated with a particular crime.

These interrelated characteristics of defendants, cases,

crimes, and the law have become the subjects of dozens of studies following in the tradition of the Chicago Jury Project. These studies have begun to amass findings that suggest that a wide inventory of marginal and nonevidentiary features of a case can influence trial verdicts. A large jury project at the London School of Economics found that admitting a defendant's previous convictions into evidence does increase the likelihood of conviction, but only if the past record contains offenses similar to that with which the defendant has been charged.[13] This pattern was given preliminary support by Kalven and Zeisel. It has been established also for a sample of Canadian trials studied by Doob and Kirschenbaum.[14] Studies by Vidmar and Hester and Smith tend to confirm Kalven and Zeisel's finding that the severity of possible punishment may affect judgment in some cases.[15]

Another important series of studies suggests that jurors admit to taking the race and class of the defendant into account in some cases.[16] We know that white-collar criminals are treated more leniently in verdicts and sentences than poor people.[17] There is evidence to suggest that, at least for some types of crimes, blacks are convicted more often and given harsher sentences than whites.[18] There is some disagreement about what systematic effect race has on verdicts, but there is consensus among researchers that when a factor like the defendant's race enters a juror's judgment in any way, the result is a breakdown of the "rule of law" principle.

Other research supports this implication that the impartiality of the rule of law is likely to be subordinated in cases in which jurors are moved by salient characteristics of the defendant or the victim. A simulation by Landy and Aronson found the "jury" recommended a shorter prison term for a defendant who was described as being happily married, employed in a good job, and a friendly person.[19] Longer sentences were given to a defendant described as an ex-convict, twice divorced, and a janitor. Another simulation by Efran found that a student "jury" sitting in judgment of a student accused of cheating was less likely to find the student guilty if he or she was physically attractive.[20] A similar study showed that adults were less inclined to respond harshly to the misconduct of an attractive child than they were to that of an unattractive child.[21] Further support for this line of research comes from the Landy and Aronson simulation. In their research they alternately pictured the crime victim as a good or bad person. Defendants tended to be punished more severely if their victims were perceived by jurors as "good" people. A similar experiment reported in Brooks and Doob found that a panel of simulated jurors thought there was more justification to convict a man who had raped a "chaste" woman than to convict a man who had raped a woman who had a history of prostitution.[22]

The main contribution of this growing collection of findings is to show the innumerable ways in which the rule of law can be compromised by juries. A lively debate exists (and has thrived for the past century) around the question of whether the jury system constitutes a threat to the rule of law. The evidence in these recent behavioral studies seems to tip the scales heavily toward the affirmative. However, a more critical jurisprudential issue lies underneath this debate. This is the matter of whether the sorts of infringements of the rule of law principle associated with the jury system are socially desirable or socially destructive. Jurists like Holmes and Pound have argued that the liberties taken by juries are important correctives that keep the notion of justice within sensible social standards.[23] Others, most notable among them Frank, have argued that the jury system threatens the notions of fairness, impartiality, and "blind justice" that are so central to the justice system.[24] Despite the accumulation of evidence in recent years, this debate has changed little.

If we are correct in assuming that adjudication involves interpreting a case in light of an implicit story model of the real world and then categorizing the resulting interpretation in terms of the legal instructions provided by the judge, we may be able to make a few small contributions to this debate. First, the routine judgments on which adjudication depends may include some crime and defendant-related understandings as a matter of course. These are not necessarily "biases" imposed by jurors; they may be integral components of their understanding of the social world and how it works. Second, if these factors figure into judgments in some cases, it is not at all clear that the "blame" for their use should be laid squarely on the jury. If jurors are oriented to working within the interpretive framework of the stories constructed by the lawyers, then we must assume that the symbols and story elements that engage these understandings were introduced by lawyers (and their witnesses) and admitted into testimony by judges. Finally, to the extent that the outcomes of justice processes are evaluated both for fairness and for correctness in terms of their congruence with implicit models of social reality, the use of crime and defendant-related understandings must reflect the patterns of social relations and beliefs current in society. To the extent that experiences and fundamental social understandings differ in society, judgments that are regarded by some members of society as unjust will occur with some frequency in ordinary social relations and in adjudication processes. Thus, it is not necessarily the case that juries either "subvert" the law or "correct" it by keeping it in line with current social outlooks. Both of these interpretations assume that the law is the central dynamic of such adjudication processes as trials. It may make more sense to think of formal justice processes as means of mobilizing dominant models of social reality as standards for judging behavior. The specific practices and socialization experiences within adjudication settings, in turn, link these implicit models of reality with the enduring symbols and principles of law and justice that assert the continuity and legitimacy of the legal system.

Although the large body of research on defendant and case-related traits has fueled some interesting discussions on such important normative questions as the status of the rule of law principle, it has shed surprisingly little light on the nature of justice processes and how they work. When all is said and done, this research has produced a legacy of dozens of variables, each of which seems to enter the reasoning of juries in a small percentage of cases. There is, however, no convincing explanation of why these variables matter, why they enter such a small percentage of cases, why they are excluded from other cases, and when they can be expected to enter any given case. In short, even though this has been, in general, a more productive area of research than lawyer and jury studies, it shares their plight of failing to link research findings to any compelling explanation of the production of justice.

Toward a Systematic Framework of Analysis

The fragmentation that has been characteristic of research on the criminal trial is beginning to receive some attention. In a major reexamination of the criminal court system, Eisenstein and Jacob note the dominant tendency to confine research designs to narrow slices of the trial and its actors.[25] They argue that this research strategy has failed to produce solid payoffs because it isolates variables from the broader contexts in which they operate. As they point out, the findings from this scattered research just don't "add up" to consistent models of adjudication processes on their own. They conclude, as we do, that "we must find more complex models which combine their effect on the final disposition of cases."[26] Their solution to the search for a more complex model is, however, a rather uneasy adaptation of an organizational metaphor to the court system. In their framework, the various actors in the trial justice system become "work groups," whose varying styles of behavior and norms explain some of the variation in case-related outcomes of court systems.

The Eisenstein and Jacob perspective helps make some sense out of the collection of scattered variables that runs throughout the current literature, but it is not an approach that tells us much about the nature of justice in justice processes. Although we are made aware of the fact that differences in bureaucratic organization among the units of a court system can affect the disposition of cases, we gain no sense of what a case represents to adjudicators, how it is presented for judgment, or on what basis it is judged. These matters would seem particularly important in a policy-oriented approach like the one pursued by Eisenstein and Jacob. If we advocate reform in the means of handling and processing cases, we should at least know what effect various reforms will have on the underlying judgment routines that are mobilized within the framework of formal organization procedures. If the symbolic forms that transmit interpretable accounts of the alleged criminal act, the cast of characters, and the circumstances surrounding their involvement are of crucial importance to those responsible for the production of justice, then we must explain how cases are presented and heard in adjudication and how these underlying justice processes are linked to the formal organizational framework of the court. This theoretical mandate holds whether we are interested in jury trials or in understanding the judgments made about cases by lawyers and judges in the process of negotiating pleas.

This gives us the occasion to summarize our perspective in a straightforward way: a trial is a set of rules for reconstructing a disputed incident in a symbolic form that allows the actions of the participants to be judged in fairly uniform fashion by (in theory at least) any judge or jury who was not witness to the incident. The rules governing formal trial procedures result in the introduction of information in ways that force jurors to concentrate particular judgment skills on a key disputed action and its immediate circumstances (as opposed, for example, to judging the character of the defendant, the opinions of judges or witnesses, etc.). Each symbolic element introduced in support of an interpretation of the central action is subject to possible disproof, resymbolization, or rejection by judge or jury as irrelevant to the interpretation of the designated central action. The judgment form that permits the most economical organization, testing, and interpretation of the information introduced within the trial format is the story.

This perspective suggests that the trial is by no means a mechanical process. Since virtually any trial lends itself to a range of case construction strategies within its overall procedural framework, and since these strategies may vary in their treatment of factors like the nature of the crime or the identity of the defendant, it makes very little sense to concentrate on the surface properties of the courtroom in isolation from their bearing on the story structure in a case. If we examine the brute connections among defendant traits, jury composition, lawyers' behavior, case outcomes, and the like, we will find only weak statistical associations with little logical basis to them. This is because the factor that determines whether or not these variables become relevant to the judgments about a case is the structure of the case itself, which guides the analysis of jurors.

Thus, various characteristics of case, crime, defendant, law, and lawyer will affect the judgment of a case only when they trigger particular understandings constrained by the strategic stories orchestrated by the lawyers. In other words, the defendant's age or marital status or race will be attributed significance by jurors when it becomes impossible *not* to resort to these bits of data as documentation for central issues in the trial stories. Likewise, if a palpable characteristic of the case, crime, defendant, or law is not relevant to testing some key claim in a defense or prosecution story, jurors would have to strain against the available interpretive devices in the case to incorporate the characteristic in their judgment. We submit that this is an unlikely possibility, given both the nature of interpretation and the strong reliance on stories as the central organizing devices in the justice process. Indeed, one of the most important functions of trial procedures is to reassure the juror that whatever information has been introduced in testimony is fair game for incorporation in the story line about the case. On the other hand, any understandings that cannot be activated directly by the story structure cannot be employed in judgment. These effects of story structure on judgment correspond to what people commonly mean by standards of fairness and objectivity in legal judgment.

This perspective suggests some modification of the naive argument that the mere presence of a black, Chicano, white-collar (etc.) defendant will bias the judgments of the typical white, middle-aged, middle-class jury. If "bias" enters the judgments in such cases, it will do so ordinarily through the lawyers who construct the cases, the witnesses who symbolize key structural elements, and the judges who rule on the admissibility of evidence and testimony. It is unlikely that these courtroom actors are any less "biased" in their involvement in a case than the jury. Moreover, the overpowering judgmental structure in a trial makes it difficult, if not impossible, for jurors to introduce bias independent of the underlying story structure in a case, or to sustain such independent bias through the deliberation process.

Our perspective does not imply that biases do not exist in formal trial processes. The story model simply makes concrete the nature and workings of those biases. The debate about whether or not there is systematic bias in the justice system is growing unproductive because there is increasing agreement (and evidence) that biases do exist, but there is little good explanation for them. Our theory suggests that certain types of bias are built into the very structure of adjudication by virtue of the sort of judgment process on which adjudication depends. When the structures of certain cases lead to verdicts that might be branded as racist, sexist, class based, and the like, we should be able to determine through story structure analysis: (1) how such social biases were triggered by the structure of the case; (2) what distinguishes these cases from seemingly identical trials in which social prejudice is a less plausible explanation for the verdict; and (3) how the conditions necessary for the jury's reliance on these characteristics were introduced into the trial. In short, we know that biases exist in the trial justice process. The interesting questions are how they become manifest and what their systematic patterns are.

We have suggested that an overriding value expressed in the legal judgment practices in criminal trials is the purchase (through story construction strategies and tactics) of some degree of freedom from the ambiguities and problematic circumstances that characterize most legal conflict situations. Participants in trials are encouraged by the formal procedures of the trial to try to reconstruct clear versions of possibly muddled real events. This opportunity to reconstruct symbolically an account of an incident implies that the portrayal of incidents in trials will often be clearer than the incident was in its natural state. The emphasis on symbolic reconstruction in trials also suggests that the general models used by jurors to interpret the competing versions of an incident will be sensitive (within the limits imposed by the evidence and its possible symbolizations) to the alternative ways in which an incident could have developed. Indeed, actual incidents that were ambiguous for those involved or that might easily have developed in other directions are vulnerable to considerable reconstruction in the trial setting. In an ideal sense this biases justice in favor of the victim of circumstances and the unwitting accomplice. Errors in judgment in this system should run in favor of the "guilty" and not against the "innocent."

Ideal states are, however, seldom attained in the real world. If the values embodied in trials are to be attained by all members of society, certain cognitive and communicative skills are required. Some individuals and groups in society may become victims of justice processes simply because they fail to share the communication and thought styles used by dominant segments of the population. In this sense, bias in the justice system results from factors that are far more subtle, and, therefore, more insidious, than overt racism or class bias. The victims of the trial justice process are people who cannot communicate in commonly accepted ways about their actions, and who, as a result of this communications gap, are also unable to explain convincingly the sense of frustration and injustice that results from their encounters with formal legal processes.

Chapter 8
Bias in the Trial Justice Process

Few social issues have produced as much debate as the controversy about whether the justice process is biased against particular groups in society. There are obvious reasons for thinking that some sort of systematic bias exists against such groups as minorities and the poor. These groups clog the justice system.[1] They receive a disproportionate share of public legal services, and they generally regard these services as inferior to those provided by private lawyers.[2] Finally, the groups who most dominate the case load of the criminal court system are judged overwhelmingly by juries and judges who do not represent the same race, class, or life-style.[3]

Despite the above prima facie conditions of bias, it has been difficult to demonstrate that large degrees of prejudicial justice do, in fact, exist in the courts. Statistical studies of the sort discussed in Chapter 7 show low correlations between variables like race or class and the outcome of cases. These low correlations do not seem to reflect the massive bias that critics of the court system claim to observe. There may, however, be problems inherent in statistical attempts to demonstrate overt social bias. For one thing, the large portion of minority and poor defendants may wipe out the variance that would be necessary to record statistical associations. Also, bias may be localized in particular demographic categories of court systems, thus making overall trends small in scale. Biases may enter all court procedures, cumulatively affecting the entire criminal process from policy decisions about what laws to enforce, to arrest procedures, to case assignments, to decisions to prosecute, and finally to decisions in the courtroom itself. If bias is spread across the entire justice process, it may be more difficult to measure it by looking only in the courts. Finally, social biases may enter the judgment of a particular case in some form other than overt racial or class prejudices.

If people made decisions on the basis of conscious social prejudice, they would have to discount virtually all the evidence and case material presented in trials. Formal cases seldom have direct references to social prejudice in them, and it would be difficult to conduct deliberations and make judgments that fully ignored the substance of cases. Most jurors seem sincere about their obligation to make fair and impartial judgments that are not influenced by their conscious prejudices. If bias enters the courtroom, it seems reasonable to suppose that it enters indirectly through the official procedures that structure jurors' judgments and communication, and not through jurors' conscious decisions to circumvent standard judgment practices in order to impose private prejudices.

Storytelling practices clear up many questions about bias in trials. First, storytelling explains how biases can enter the courtroom through formal legal procedures. Second, stories show that biases that are not based primarily on conscious social prejudice can, nonetheless, be weighted heavily against particular social groups. Third, the ways in which stories are presented and reconstructed in trials indicate that social biases will be more likely to enter some cases than others, independent of defendant characteristics and juror prejudices. This selective entry of bias through case structure explains why social bias is not necessarily constant across otherwise similar crimes, defendants, and juries. Finally, bias introduced in story construction helps to illuminate the "carriers" of bias in the justice process. The storytelling perspective suggests that judges, lawyers, and witnesses must share the responsibility with jurors for biases in the courtroom. In fact, the sort of bias that we have identified is part and parcel of the formal justice process.

How Bias Enters Legal Judgments

When people say that trials are objective and impartial means of producing legal judgments, what they really mean is that trials rely on a standardized means of packaging and analyzing information: the story. The reconstruction of evidence in the form of a story does not guarantee that the truth will emerge in a trial, nor does it ensure that all the possible interpretations of evidence will be considered. Storytelling simply provides defendants with a means of reconstructing an incident to their best advantage and presenting the reconstruction to an audience who will judge it according to its plausibility. In principle this feature of trials ought to provide a universal safeguard against false or misguided accusation and conviction. In fact, however, this protection of the justice process only holds if all parties in an adjudication have the same capacity to present and judge stories.

There are two ways in which systematic biases might result from differences in storytelling practices. First, some people may lack shared cognitive routines for presenting information in story-coded forms. The inability to produce a conventional story would leave individuals vulnerable to having truthful accounts of their actions rejected. Second, even the construction of a coherent story may not guarantee a just outcome if the teller and the audience do not share the norms, experiences, and assumptions necessary to draw connections among story elements. People who have different understandings about society and its norms may disagree about the plausibility of a story. If legal judgment is not just a process of adding up the "facts" in a case, then social and demographic differences between jurors may be significant. If legal facts are reconstructed as stories whose plausibility depends on understandings drawn from experience, then jurors who come from different social worlds may disagree about the meaning and the plausibility of the same stories.

Although storytelling skills are among the most broadly

shared cognitive and linguistic abilities, there is reason to suspect that group differences may exist in the means of representing social behavior. For example, Labov has suggested that ethnic groups like blacks living in fairly insulated environments may develop separate vernaculars that differ from standard language usage in both syntax and vocabulary.[4] Since language is essential to story construction both in the process of coding story elements for proper assembly and in the process of setting up inferences, significant differences in patterns of language usage may place users of a minority language at a disadvantage when critical legal judgments are made by users of a majority language.

While the distinction in vernaculars may bias the justice process against particular ethnic groups in society, another cognitive-linguistic difference may cut across society along lines of class or socioeconomic status. The cultural and educational experiences of particular social and economic groups (e.g., middle and upper economic strata) may equip them with more complex cognitive and communicative capacities. In his research in England, Bernstein has found a difference between what he calls the "formal language" of the middle class and the "public language" of the working class.[5] Formal language is characterized by an elaborated language code that permits easy abstraction, broad categorical operations, and wide degrees of descriptive freedom. Such symbolic operations are essential for the broad reconstruction of events in standard story forms as defined in Chapter 3. A public language, by contrast, is restricted in vocabulary and characterized by grammatical simplicity. Public languages with their restricted language codes limit the range of descriptive terms, restrict the capacity to abstract, produce fragmented accounts, and are more dependent on contextual factors for meanings than formal languages. Formal languages are the languages of institutions. Public languages place their users at a disadvantage when communicating in formal institutional settings that emphasize explicit linguistic skills and restrict the ability of individuals to rely on the informal tonal, gestural, kinesthetic, and social context factors that contribute to communication in restricted language codes.

The courtroom is a classic example of a setting that places speakers of an elaborated code at an advantage because of their ability to reconstruct information more broadly through stories. The impact of formal political and legal processes on language and cognition has been noted by Bloch in his work on ritualized communication processes.[6] The formal processes of political and legal institutions limit the ways in which participants can express themselves, and place individuals who have certain cognitive and linguistic skills at a competitive political advantage.[7]

If different groups in American society use different vernaculars or language codes, then some groups will suffer disadvantages in formal legal processes that emphasize expression and judgment in terms of a particular code. What may surface in quantitative research as weak statistical links between variables like race or class and case outcomes may be a much broader and more subtle bias based on communication styles. This bias may be even more insidious than overt race or class prejudices because it does not operate systematically against all members of the affected groups in every case, yet members of these groups stand a higher chance of suffering bias in any given trial. Moreover, if bias operates through storytelling, it would be difficult in most cases to point to overt prejudice at work, yet differences in communication styles in trials may produce effects that are every bit as damaging and discriminatory as overt prejudice.

A number of factors explain why communication and judgment bias in trials will not apply to all members of affected groups in every trial. Some speakers of nonstandard languages or minority language codes may have the capacity to switch codes, and, thereby, represent events in forms that are familiar to the average juror. Also, certain lawyers may be particularly sensitive to the differences between the cognitive styles of witnesses and jurors, and exercise much more careful control over some testimony than would ordinarily be necessary. In a surprisingly large number of the cases that we observed, however, we were struck by the fact that a whole lineup of witnesses for certain defendants produced testimony that was hard to reconstruct in standard story form, while prosecution witnesses (particularly police officers and experts) delivered accounts that fit easily into coherent stories. Lawyers for defendants whose witnesses produced inadequate stories seemed either to accept the state of affairs as probable evidence of guilt, or were simply powerless to impose other cognitive structures on successive lines of testimony.

The point of this discussion is not to suggest that one form of describing or constructing accounts of social behavior is superior to another. However, the average participant in the justice process, whether judge or juror, expects testimony to conform to particular story criteria. When these criteria are not met, the presumption is not that the speaker merely uses a different language code or structures accounts differently. The presumption is that the speaker's version of an incident is suspect.

Very few white, adult, middle-class witnesses (and defendants) fail to provide testimony that can be translated into standard story forms intelligible to the average white middle-class juror. The effective consequence of this pattern is a bias in the trial justice system against members of subcultures. As mentioned above, this bias is not based on conscious prejudice, nor, because of variations in lines of testimony, case strategies, lawyer sensitivity and skill, and defendant capacity to switch codes, does it operate across the board in class terms. Nevertheless, this bias is clearly weighted against particular social groups, and it is more serious even than overt prejudice because it is a result of the very structure of legal judgments in society.

Justice in Different Social Worlds

One reason the problem of bias in the trial justice process is so elusive is that bias does not result solely from the inability to deliver testimony in standard story form. To get interpreted properly, a story also requires that the teller and listener share knowledge about the world. As pointed out earlier, bias can result when an adequate story is told, but the listener lacks the norms, knowledge, or assumptions to draw the inferences intended by the teller. The internal consistency and the significance of stories can be damaged if listeners and tellers live in different social worlds and hold different norms and beliefs about social behavior.

Thus even the cognitive and communicational capacity to deliver testimony in standard story form does not guarantee that all individuals will be judged equally. In addition to constructing a recognizable story, the defense must produce a story that is based on experiences familiar to those who will judge it (or, if the defense strategy is to attack the prosecution story, the attack must be based on assumptions familiar to the jurors). Bias that stems from divergence in the norms and understandings necessary to interpret stories further ensures that group disadvantage will not be manifest in every case. Only when the key interpretive issues in a case happen to fall outside the range of shared social experience between teller and listener will judgments become arbitrary and distorted. There is good reason, then, why not all cases involving minority or poor defendants and white middle-class jurors will result in discriminatory judgment practices. Some cases will produce standard stories that elicit shared criteria for making connections and drawing inferences. Other cases will either fail to produce coherent story strategies or result in stories that have no plausible interpretations consistent with the social understandings of judge or jurors.

Stories that elicit different interpretations are among the most painful things to observe in the courtroom. When the defense manages to construct a plausible story only to discover that the jury lacks the experiences necessary to understand it, the stark reality of injustice becomes clear. For example, Swett observed the case of a young black accused of first degree murder. His defense was based on the claim that the victim had been the aggressor and that the killing was self-defense. This story required the construction of a plausible basis for the victim's aggressive behavior. The defense attempted to show that the deceased had displayed his hostility to the defendant even before the defendant was attacked physically. The deceased, according to one witness, had "put him in the dozens." This phrase refers to a ritualized form of verbal aggression that occurred in that particular subculture. When the defense lawyer attempted to clarify this key element in the story for the benefit of the jury, the prosecution successfully blocked all testimony from the witnesses on the grounds that they were not semantics experts. Swett observed that "as a consequence, both judge and jury were left completely in the dark on at least one crucial point in the case."[8]

Our sample of trials included numerous cases containing key story elements that would not hold the same meanings to members of different subcultures or social worlds. For example, a murder trial centered around the story of a black defendant who entered a "white" bar to have a drink with his brother. The two men sat down and ordered beers. The defendant claimed that after the bartender left the beers, he was fooling around and grabbed a bottle of wine from behind the bar and told his brother that he needed a little chaser. The next thing he knew, he was attacked by the bartender and several other patrons, and the shooting followed. The bartender claimed that the man was in the act of stealing the wine. A key issue involved the interpretation of the act of grabbing the bottle of wine. The struggle over the interpretation of this action was focused on the norms applying to touching private property without the permission of the owner—norms that may not have applied in the defendant's subculture. The prosecution introduced these norms clearly during cross-examination of the defendant, and the defendant could do little more than admit that he had learned his lesson about property norms in a costly way:

Prosecution: Do you normally reach behind the counter and pull bottles of wine up?
Defense: I object, Your Honor.

The Court: Objection overruled.
Defendant: No, I don't. I don't know why I done that, really. It was just the mood I was in. I don't know what was wrong with me. Normally I don't do that.
Prosecution: Do you feel that that would have been an improper action on your part under the circumstances, to be playing with their bottle of wine?
Defendant: I know better than that now, yeah, than to touch wine in somebody's place.
Prosecution: As a matter of fact, didn't you know better than to do that at that time, also?
Defendant: I didn't think that all that would happen, something like that.

It is clear from this exchange that the prosecutor and the judge presumed that the norm that applied to this key element in the story was a universal one. Not only was the objection of the defense attorney overruled, but the defendant's claims not to have "known better" are easily understood as a lie to conceal his intention to steal the wine. As Swett's analysis implied, the justice process is not only blind to significant differences in the realities of different groups of society, but in a trial formal legal procedures are often employed to keep any hint of these differences out of the developing case. Since trials are understood by participants as simple forums for presenting the objective facts in a case, the justice process would be called in question if facts were shown to be anchored in quite different realities. Since jurors can employ only their own knowledge and experience in making judgments, any effective demonstration of the social relativity of facts and norms would attack the very basis of legal judgment. If jurors must use their own norms and social knowledge to interpret stories, any challenge to the "obvious" meanings of behavior would either leave jurors incapable of understanding the issues in a case or unable to render a confident and seemingly objective judgment about those issues. Thus the uncomfortable paradox of the legal judgment process is that any formal acknowledgment of different social realities would shatter the practices through which jurors think they make fair and objective judgments. In other words, attempts to remedy bias would undermine the basis of legal judgment.

It is no accident that in the murder case involving the alleged theft of the bottle of wine, the prosecutor was successful in blocking any plausible normative support for the idea that the defendant was just playing around and, therefore, that the chain of events leading to the killing was the unfortunate result of the bartender's misperception. As a result of the inability of the defense to introduce any other normatively acceptable interpretation of the defendant's behavior, the judge refused to instruct the jury that it could also consider the possibility of manslaughter instead of homicide. Following a defense argument that a manslaughter consideration was justified by the defendant's own version of what happened, the judge replied, "I am not aware of any evidence which would support a manslaughter instruction. Proceed." Indeed, as long as the judge refused to consider the defendant's behavior prior to the shooting in light of any norms other than those pertaining to the sanctity of private property, the only possible interpretation was that the defendant shot someone after he had been caught trying to steal a bottle of wine.

We could cite dozens of other examples of divergent interpretations of the same story in a trial, but the point does not need further embellishment. Overt social discrimination in the court system is difficult to document because it is seldom based on blatant social prejudice. Bias operates more often in the form of differences in norms and understandings between different social groups, making it difficult to understand the meaning of circumstances surrounding actions or the meaning of responses to those circumstances. Even these differences will not enter every case because there is almost always some area of overlapping social experience between members of different groups, and the key issues in a particular case may fall within the range of shared understandings. The very existence of some degree of overlap in experiences and understandings makes the sort of bias we are talking about all the more troublesome. In those cases in which most of the inferences make perfect sense within the range of familiar and shared social understandings, it is all the more tempting for judges, jurors, and observers to reject alternative interpretations for the few deviant story elements as irrelevant, or, worse yet, as evidence of fabrication.

Looking to the Future

The use of storytelling in the judgment process is based on the necessary assumption that experience and meaning are universal. In place of recognizing legitimate differences in the interpretation of social experience, jurors more often are compelled to regard unfamiliar story elements or dissonant interpretations as signs of guilt. When key elements in a case are anchored in different social worlds, defendants may be found guilty simply by reason of their social experiences and their communication styles. The important question arising from this state of affairs is whether anything can be done to correct biased judgment in trials.

The most obvious remedy for the problem of bias would be to introduce judges, lawyers, witnesses, and jurors to the idea that social norms and understandings are anchored in experience and, therefore, may differ from one group to another. This is an unrealistic remedy for the obvious reason that it would entail a change in basic cultural judgment practices. It may, however, be possible for trained experts who recognize the relativity of legal judgment to try to shape the aspects of cases most affected by differences in storytelling.

Some efforts by social scientists to intervene in trials have come close to the corrective measures that would follow logically from the storytelling perspective. For example, a team of social scientists working on the trial of Joan Little were able to avert potentially damaging bias in the case by documenting a set of dubious understandings common among residents in the case's original jurisdiction. Little was a black woman held prisoner in the Beaufort County jail in Washington, North Carolina. She killed a jailer who she claimed had assaulted and raped her. It was clear that a possible focus of the prosecution case could involve the question of whether she had lured the jailer into her cell with the intention of killing him and making an escape from the jail. John McConahay and other social scientists involved in the case were concerned that whites in the small and provincial community surrounding Washington shared certain beliefs about blacks that would favor the prosecution's case. A survey of Beaufort County residents vindicated these concerns. Respondents to the survey were asked two questions that might have become central to judging the prosecution case: "Do you believe that black women have lower morals than white women? Do you believe that black people are more violent than white people?"

A full 63 percent of the sample responded yes to both questions. By contrast, a sample drawn from a larger urban county in the same state registered only a 35 percent yes response to both questions.[9] These startling differences provided the basis for a successful motion for a change of venue—a move that probably contributed to the defendant's eventual acquittal.

The Little case and others like it are encouraging signs that biases in the justice process can be corrected. Unfortunately, our optimism is limited by some factors that distinguish political trials and other well publicized cases from routine cases involving minority and poor defendants. For one thing, few defendants have the benefit of a team of trained experts to assess the possible bias in a case. In addition, it is often difficult to anticipate the ways in which differences in social understandings will affect the judgment of a case. The Little case involved issues that were relatively easy to anticipate and, more important, that touched on fairly obvious social beliefs. Related to the last point is the crucial fact that the social beliefs recorded among residents of Beaufort County were easily identified as overt racial prejudices and stereotypes. Clear evidence of blatant prejudice is something that the court system can attempt to correct. However, much of the routine bias that enters criminal trials through storytelling cannot be classified as explicit prejudice. What, for example, would an average judge do if it was demonstrated that the majority of jurors in the jurisdiction of the murder trial reported earlier by Swett did not understand the significance of putting someone "in the dozens"? Would this be regarded as prejudicial to the defendant's case? Probably not. Yet the absence of understandings about key elements of the defense case, or the presence of understandings that favor the interpretation of the prosecution case can be just as damaging to a defendant as blatant racism.

Two overriding considerations make the elimination of social bias from trials an unlikely prospect. First, the whole inventory of divergent social understandings between defendants and other courtroom actors would be impossible to document. Second, even if differences in social outlook could be documented, most of them could not be regarded as sources of bias without acknowledging the inherent subjectivity and relativity of legal judgment. The overwhelming popular commitment to the myths of fairness and objectivity in the justice process virtually prohibits the official recognition of any but the most blatant social prejudices. Indeed, storytelling can sustain the conscious presumption of objectivity and fairness in the legal judgment process only if participants in trials presume the existence of a broad uniformity in communication skills and social experience.

The dubious presumption that uniformity in communication and social experience exists across trial participants results in a painful impasse between different groups participating in the justice system. Those who discover that the best reconstructions of their cases have fallen on insensitive ears may feel that they have suffered the harsh effects of social prejudice. Yet the way in which this "prejudice" operates permits the majority of white middle-class participants in the court system to deny its existence. Indeed, these denials are probably sincere and supportable in the sense that it is usually hard to locate signs of overt social prejudices operating in trials. Thus the typical reaction to charges of prejudice is to dismiss them as self-serving political rhetoric.

Just as participants' understanding of the issues in cases may diverge because of differences in communication styles or social experiences, so may perceptions of the degrees and the causes of injustice in trials differ for the same reasons. The same factors that produce different interpretations of stories result in different understandings about justice and injustice, as illustrated in the following exchange between a black defendant who was convicted of larceny and the white judge who presided over the trial and the sentencing. The outcome of the trial hinged to a large degree on differences in norms that applied to common everyday behavior. The defendant probably did not recognize the specific divergence in norms that made his story sound implausible to the jury. Instead, he interpreted the verdict as the product of overt racial prejudice. The judge who listened to the defendant's assertion of racial bias in the trial could not, of course, see any evidence of overt prejudice. He felt compelled, as a result, to defend the trial process as fair and impartial:

Defendant: I have done a lot of growing up this last month since the jury brought in the verdict of guilty. . . . I always believe I could play any game if I know the rules, so I prided myself in knowing the rules of the establishment and live by the rules. But now I find that there are different rules for blacks. If I have black witnesses, no white jury will believe them. If I have evidence, no white jury will believe it. They would rather believe a white prosecutor's statement that— anyone can see this is the signature of a seventeen year old. I have become a militant. In the past month I am believing for the first time that our court system is not to protect the black but is meant to hurt him.

Judge: I don't agree with the statement Mr. P___ has made with respect to the system. I recognize there are imperfections in it; there are injustices that occur . . . but I do not feel that this offense can in any way be explained on the basis of prejudice by everyone involved in the system from the initial arrest by a white officer to the prosecution by a white prosecutor to the trial of facts by a white jury to the last role that I have to play as a white judge. I personally would much prefer to see the minority members of the community represented better throughout the entire system and in the police department and in the prosecution's office and on juries and as judges sitting in the court but for one reason or another that simply is not a fact. I think today that most people try to understand their own background and the background of other people and try to accommodate the differences and understand one another.

Just as social differences affected the verdict in the case, so the inability to communicate about those differences left the participants with irreconcilable understandings about the justice process itself. Perhaps the most important contribution of the storytelling perspective is that it explains how legal judgment works and, at the same time, shows how justice fails.

Notes

1. For an illuminating development of these ideas, see the following works by Kenneth Burke: *A Grammar of Motives* (Berkeley: University of California Press, 1969); *A Rhetoric of Motives* (Berkeley: University of California Press, 1969); *A Philosophy of Literary Form* (Berkeley: University of California Press, 1973).

2. This methodology is described in more detail later. An introduction to the methodological principles that guided our investigation can be obtained by reading such sources as: Egon Bittner, "The Concept of Organization," *Social Research* 32 (1965):239–255; Aaron Cicourel, *Method and Measurement in Sociology* (New York: Free Press, 1964); Cicourel, "Ethnomethodology," in *Current Trends in Linguistics*, vol. 12, ed. Thomas S. Sebeok (London: Mouton, 1972); Harold Garfinkel, *Studies in Ethnomethodology* (Englewood Cliffs, N.J.: Prentice-Hall, 1967); Peter McHugh, *Defining the Situation* (Indianapolis: Bobbs-Merrill, 1968); Alfred Schutz, *The Collected Papers: I. The Problem of Social Reality* (The Hague: Martinus Nijhoff, 1962); D. Lawrence Wieder, "On Meaning by Rule," in *Understanding Everyday Life*, ed. Jack Douglas (Chicago: Aldine, 1970); Thomas P. Wilson, "Normative and Interpretive Paradigms in Sociology" in *Understanding Everyday Life*, ed. Douglas; and Don H. Zimmerman and Melvin Pollner, "The Everyday World as a Phenomenon," in *Understanding Everyday Life*, ed. Douglas.

3. We are particularly indebted to the judge who presided on this case. Without his considerable efforts, the taping simply would not have been possible. Since we have adopted a blanket

policy of anonymity for our contacts and informants, we extend our personal gratitude, but we feel constrained to forgo a formal acknowledgment.

4. The transcripts were selected from the file of cases that had been heard on appeal during a period of six months. Three criteria were used in selecting the cases. First, we wanted examples of the various types of cases (narcotics, murder, burglary, etc.) that we had observed in the courtroom. Second, we selected only those cases that had been appealed on grounds that would not have been reflected directly (insofar as the jury was concerned) in the conduct of the trial. Thus, we selected cases that had been appealed on grounds of an interpretation of the law or a judge's ruling on the admissibility of evidence or testimony during a preliminary hearing. We did not include cases in which the grounds for appeal either represented (or stemmed from) significant disruptions or improprieties during the course of the trial. Third, we selected only those cases for which complete transcripts (more correctly, "statements of fact") existed.

Chapter 2

1. John M. Roberts, "Oaths, Autonomic Ordeals, and Power," *American Anthropologist* 67 (December 1965):187. See also K. N. Llewelyn and E. A. Hoebel, *The Cheyenne Way* (Norman: University of Oklahoma Press, 1941), p. 153.

2. R. F. Barton, "Procedures among the Ifugao," in *Law and Warfare*, ed. Paul Bohannon (Garden City, N.Y.: Natural History Press, 1969).

3. Ralph Linton, *The Tanala: A Tribe in Madagascar* (Chicago: Publications of the Field Museum of Natural History, 1933), pp. 156–157.

4. Laura Nader, "Styles of Court Procedures: To Make the Balance," in her *Law in Culture and Society* (Chicago: Aldine, 1969).

5. Paul Vinogradoff, *Common Sense in Law* (New York: Henry Holt and Co., 1914), p. 88.

6. John C. Messenger, Jr., "The Role of Proverbs in a Nigerian Judicial System," *Southwestern Journal of Anthropology* 15 (1959):64–73. Evidence of the centrality of proverbs in Anang communication is demonstrated in the very origins of the name "Anang": "Neighboring Ibo gave the Anang their name, the term denoted 'ability to speak wittily yet meaningfully upon any occasion.'" Ibid., p. 64.

7. Max Gluckman, *The Judicial Process among the Barotse of Northern Rhodesia* (Manchester: Manchester University Press, 1955), pp. 82–83.

8. Gluckman has come under considerable attack for his use of this exogenous ("etic") concept of the "reasonable man" to describe culture-bound ("emic") ideas. His defense of this usage is credibly organized around two points: first, his approach is little different from that of other ethnographers who have *analyzed* the social practices of other cultures and, thus, have had to find "analogous" foreign language in terms to present the case to nonnative audiences; and, second, he did not, as some of his critics seem to imply, assume that the standards of reasonableness are the same across cultures. He uses the term "reasonable man" only as an analytical concept to convey the idea that a unique set of Barotse norms enters the justice process and functions in ways that are similar to other standards of reasonable behavior that operate in other cultures. See Gluckman, "Concepts in the Comparative Study of Tribal Law," in *Law in Culture and Society*, ed. Nader.

While we find Gluckman's defense of the "reasonable man" concept acceptable, we think that the entire emic versus etic debate has missed the most important issue at stake. The truly problematic question, it seems to us, is not *whether* particular standards of reasonableness are used or differences in substance weigh against similarities in function, but how it is that participants in adjudication know implicitly how to select and apply relevant judgment standards. This latter question makes it possible to point to broad functional similarities across cultures but to preserve at the same time important differences in judgment practices and the justice principles revealed in those practices.

9. Gluckman, *Judicial Process*, p. 93.

Chapter 3

1. This chapter is adapted from W. Lance Bennett, "Storytelling in Criminal Trials: A Model of Social Judgment," *Quarterly Journal of Speech* 64 (February 1968):1–22. Permission to reprint this material has been granted by the Speech Communication Association.

2. On the importance of causal coding for interpretation, see Roger C. Schank, "The Structure of Episodes in Memory," in *Representation and Understanding: Studies in Cognitive Science*, ed. Daniel G. Bobrow and Allan M. Collins (New York: Academic Press, 1975).

3. L. Newmark and M. W. Bloomfield, *A Linguistic Introduction to the History of English* (New York: Alfred A. Knopf, 1963), pp. 70–71.

4. Plot devices must be distinguished from basic interpretive structure in stories. Plot techniques may thoroughly rearrange the sequence of events in a story, but the basic rules for interpreting a story allow the listener to recombine the information in familiar and more readily accessible form. In this way, a storyteller can use plot techniques to distort, or otherwise call attention to, particular features of the incident, yet still produce an interpretable account. In cases in which the plot techniques seem to render the underlying story unrecoverable, it is unlikely that an adequate story has been told at all. Although we apply this maxim to nonfiction stories, a good illustration of it comes from the realm of fiction. The literary genre that critics have termed "postmodern fiction" creates special interpretive prob-

lems for readers and critics alike. These problems result from plot-story ambiguities. For example, Robbe-Grillet's works *In the Labyrinth* and *Plan for a Revolution in New York* contain detailed accounts of realistic situations in which scenes and characters are continuous, time appears to progress, and actions seem to be building toward some climax. Despite these appearances, coherent simple stories cannot be recovered from the plot mazes of these novels. This is because the actions and situations do not build toward a mutually defining relationship, not because the plots are too complex. For an analysis of this phenomenon, see Bruce Morrisette, "Post-Modern Generative Fiction: Novel and Film," *Critical Inquiry* 2 (Winter 1975): 253–262. Indeed, if an account conforms to basic story rules, it is virtually impossible to complicate the plot to a degree that would foil a careful listener. For example, a "traditional novel" like *Tristram Shandy* is open to coherent interpretation despite a maddening array of plot distractions. In his analysis of *Tristram Shandy*, Victor Shklovsky provides a succinct summary of the general point being made here. "The idea of *plot* is all too often confused with the description of events—with what I propose provisionally to call the *story*." See Shklovsky, "Sterne's *Tristram Shandy*: Stylistic Commentary," in *Russian Formalist Criticism: Four Essays*, ed. L. T. Lemon and M. Reis (Lincoln: University of Nebraska Press, 1965), p. 57.

5. Vladimir Propp, *Morphology of the Folktale* (Austin: University of Texas Press, 1968). In this scheme the significance of a story is a function of the relationship between the central action and the developing situation. Although he doesn't specify how these "functions" are calculated, he uses the term in an analytical sense: "Function is understood as an act of a character, defined from the point of view of the significance for the court of action." Ibid., p. 21.

6. Harold Garfinkel, "Common Sense Knowledge of Social Structures: The Documentary Method of Interpretation with Lay and Professional Fact Finding," in his *Studies in Ethnomethodology* (Englewood Cliffs, N.J.: Prentice-Hall, 1967). Aaron

Cicourel, *Cognitive Sociology: Language and Meaning in Social Inter-actions* (New York: Free Press, 1974), Chapter 4.

7. Even though trials are public record, concern about any further stigmatization of the defendants in these cases underlie our decision not to reveal either the names of the participants or the titles of the cases from our sample.

8. Harvey Sacks, "On the Analyzability of Stories by Chil-dren," in *Directions in Sociolinguistics: The Ethnography of Com-munication*, ed. J. J. Gumpers and D. Hymes (New York: Holt, Rinehart and Winston, 1972).

9. A more technical discussion of Sacks's general point can be found in John D. Bransford and Nancy S. McCarrell, "A Sketch of a Cognitive Approach to Comprehension: Some Thoughts about What It Means to Comprehend," in *Cognition and the Sym-bolic Processes*, ed. W. B. Weimer and D. S. Palermo (Hillsdale, N.J.: Lawrence Erlbaum Associates, 1974). Their discussion con-tains many excellent illustrations.

10. Roger C. Schank and Robert P. Abelson, *Scripts, Plans, Goals, and Understanding: An Inquiry into Human Knowledge Struc-tures* (Hillsdale, N.J.: Lawrence Erlbaum Associates, 1977).

11. Why didn't the defense suggest this categorization and its related normative connection? The defense attorney apparently rejected a brainwashing defense on grounds that the issues in-volved were too complex for most jurors to grasp. (See any American news magazine for the weeks of February 22, March 1, and March 8, 1976.) Although this reasoning seems dubious in retrospect, the lawyer was correct in assuming that the jurors could understand a relationship of coercion between people. The category "coercion" did lead jurors to the unequivocal ap-plication of empirical and normative understandings to the case. When considered in terms of story structure, however, there were serious inconsistencies among the connections. These inconsistencies, when compared to a consistent prosecu-tion account, led the jury to determine beyond a reasonable doubt that the defendant had participated in a willful theft of property by means of force.

12. See Kenneth Burke, *Permanence and Change* (Indianapolis: Bobbs-Merrill, 1954); and *A Grammar of Motives* (Berkeley: University of California Press, 1969).

13. See, for example: Erving Goffman, *Frame Analysis* (New York: Harper and Row, 1974); Roger C. Schank, "The Structure of Episodes in Memory," in *Representation and Understanding*, ed. Bobrow and Collins; Marvin Minsky, "A Framework for Representing Knowledge," in *The Psychology of Computer Vision*, ed. P. Winston (New York: McGraw-Hill, 1975); Benjamin J. Kuipers, "A Frame for Frames," in *Representation and Understanding*, ed. Bobrow and Collins; Terry Winograd, "Frame Representations and Declarative/Procedural Controversy," in *Representation and Understanding*, ed. Bobrow and Collins; and Robert P. Abelson, "Concepts for Representing Mundane Reality in Plans," in *Representation and Understanding*, ed. Bobrow and Collins.

14. See Harold Garfinkel, "Some Rules of Correct Decisions That Jurors Respect," in his *Studies in Ethnomethodology* for a list of the formal attributes that jurors attach to their decisions.

15. The idea that judgments and recollections are often liberal reconstructions of real events has had a long history in philosophy and psychology. Among the classical statements is Jerome Bruner's essay, "Beyond the Information Given," reprinted in *Beyond the Information Given: Studies in the Psychology of Knowing*, ed. Jeremy Anglin (New York: W. W. Norton, 1973). The constructionist perspective is gaining increasing prominence in current theories of memory. See, for example: Elizabeth F. Loftus, "Reconstructing Memory: The Incredible Eyewitness," *Psychology Today* 8 (1974):116–119; Elizabeth F. Loftus and J. C. Palmer, "Reconstruction of Automobile Destruction: An Example of the Interaction between Language and Memory," *Journal of Verbal Learning and Verbal Behavior* 13 (October 1974):585–589; and Elizabeth F. Loftus, "Leading Questions and the Eyewitness Report," *Cognitive Psychology* 7 (October 1975):560–572.

Chapter 4

1. To the extent that such an association exists in the real world, it is owing to the sense of moral obligation on the part of storytellers to tell the truth and the propensity of audiences to believe them on faith. As our results show, such an association is not attributable to any ability of audiences to differentiate a true story from one that is told well but is false, or to recognize the truth in an inadequately structured account.

2. Storytellers did not record guesses about their own stories. Also, to make sure that the act of telling a story did not have an effect on the ability of storytellers-cum-audience members to judge the truth status of other stories, we compared the guesses of storytellers and nonstorytellers. There was no discernible difference in the pattern of guesses.

3. The model that we describe below weights the connections to the central action twice as much as the peripheral connections. This weighting factor is somewhat arbitrary. We could have chosen a factor of 3, 4, 5, and so on. Further empirical work will shed light on the fine points of the model. Our interest at this stage in the development of the theory is only to see whether we are correct in the general assumption that connections to the central action weight most heavily in judging stories.

4. See Harold Garfinkel, *Studies in Ethnomethodology* (Englewood Cliffs, N.J.: Prentice-Hall, 1967).

5. Roger C. Schank and Robert P. Abelson, *Scripts, Plans, Goals, and Understanding: An Inquiry into Human Knowledge Structures* (Hillsdale, N.J.: Lawrence Erlbaum Associates, 1977).

6. It is clear that a statement about being invited to a birthday party that was not followed by some account of what happened at the party (or of the significance of the invitation) could not be classified as a story. Stories are, by definition, devices that constrain a meaning for some communicationally important action or event. A group of phrases that suggests no mutual significance, that has no common bearing on some central action, or

that suggests no development of action cannot be called a story. See Chapter 3 for an elaboration of this argument.

7. This does not mean that the central action must be related in the active tense. For example, in "The Birthday Party," the central action is described in the passive tense. However, the phrase "At the party we had" depicts the act of having or eating dinner.

8. These gaps could have been filled easily with elements that would have established the significance of the meal and diminished the importance of the birthday party setting in reaching an interpretation. For example, the storyteller could have added: "All of us at the party were impoverished students, and the meal was the best one we had eaten in months," or "Peggy is a gourmet cook, and since she had been talking about this meal for weeks it was the high point of the evening."

9. Since the stories were told in three sessions to audiences of different sizes, the first decision that had to be made was whether there were serious differences in the data that would require a separate analysis for each group, or whether the data could be combined for a single analysis. After determining that the groups did not differ significantly along any of the measured variables, the data were pooled. However, because of the different audience sizes in the three sessions, our analysis of story credibility could not be based on the absolute number of audience guesses about each story. The measure of credibility had to control for the size of the audience.

Chapter 5

1. Murray Kempton, *The Briar Patch* (New York: E. P. Dutton, 1973), p. 140.

2. In addition to Kempton, see: Stephen G. Chaberski, "Inside the New York Panther Trial," *Civil Liberties Review* 1 (Fall 1973):111–115; Edward Kennebeck, *Juror Number Four* (New York: W. W. Norton, 1973).

3. Kennebeck, *Juror Number Four*, pp. 124–126.

4. Mary Timothy, *Jury Woman* (Palo Alto, Cal.: Emty Press, 1974).

5. Ibid., pp. 80–81.

Chapter 6

1. Portions of this chapter are reprinted from W. Lance Bennett, "Rhetorical Transformations of Evidence in Criminal Trials: Creating Grounds for Legal Judgment," *Quarterly Journal of Speech* 65 (October 1979):311–323, with permission of the Speech Communication Association.

2. Quoted in A. Averbach and C. Price, eds., *The Verdicts Were Just* (New York: David McKay, 1961), pp. 180–181.

3. Gerald Abrahams, *The Legal Mind: An Approach to the Dynamics of Advocacy* (London: H. F. L. Publishers, 1954), p. 28.

Chapter 7

1. Francis L. Wellman, *The Art of Cross Examination* (New York: Collier Macmillan, 1903), pp. 24–25, 28.

2. Ibid., p. 43.

3. See, for example: Gerald Abrahams, *The Legal Mind: An Approach to the Dynamics of Advocacy* (London: H. F. L. Publishers, 1954); A. Averbach and C. Price, eds., *The Verdicts Were Just* (New York: David McKay, 1961); and L. W. Lake, *How to Win Lawsuits before Juries* (Englewood Cliffs, N.J.: Prentice-Hall, 1954).

4. *Time*, March 1, 1976, p. 16.

5. *Newsweek*, March 1, 1976, p. 25.

6. Ibid., p. 28.

7. See, for example: Joan B. Kessler, "An Empirical Study of Six and Twelve Member Jury Decision-Making Processes," *University of Michigan Journal of Law Reform* 6 (1972–1973):712–734;

and L. R. Mills, "Six and Twelve Member Juries: An Empirical Study of Trial Results," *University of Michigan Journal of Law Reform* 6 (1972–1973):671–711.

8. F. L. Strodtbeck, R. M. Jones, and C. Hawkins, "Social Status in Jury Deliberations," *American Sociological Review* 22 (1957):713–719.

9. F. L. Strodtbeck, "Social Process, the Law, and Jury Functioning," in *Law and Sociology*, ed. W. M. Williams (New York: Free Press, 1962).

10. See, for example, H. Mitchell and D. Byrne, "Effects of Jurors' Attitudes and Authoritarianism on Judicial Decisions," *Journal of Personality and Social Psychology* 25 (1973):123–129; and Jan Schulman, Phillip Shaver, Robert Colman, Barbara Emrich, and Richard Christie, "Recipe for a Jury," *Psychology Today* 6 (May 1973):37ff.

11. Harry Kalven and Hans Zeisel, *The American Jury* (Boston: Little, Brown and Co., 1966).

12. Ibid., p. 296.

13. London School of Economics Jury Project, "Juries and the Rules of Evidence," *Criminal Law Review* (April 1973):208–223.

14. A. N. Doob and H. M. Kirschenbaum, "Some Empirical Evidence on the Effect of Section 12 of the Canada Evidence Act on the Accused," *Criminal Law Quarterly* 15 (1972):88–96.

15. Neil Vidmar, "Effects of Decision Alternatives on the Verdicts and Social Perceptions of Simulated Jurors," *Journal of Personality and Social Psychology* 22 (1972):211–218. R. K. Hester and R. E. Smith, "Effects of a Mandatory Death Penalty on the Decisions of Simulated Jurors as a Function of the Heinousness of the Crime," *Journal of Criminal Justice* 1 (1973):319–326.

16. See, for example: H. A. Bullock, "Significance of the Racial Factor in the Length of Prison Sentences," *Journal of Criminal Law, Criminology, and Police Science* 52 (1961):411–415; D. W. Broeder, "The Negro in Court," *Duke University Law Journal* 19 (1965):19–31; T. P. Thornberry, "Race, Socioeconomic Status, and Sentencing in the Juvenile Justice System," *Journal of Criminal Law and Criminology* 64 (1973):90–98.

17. William J. Chambliss, introduction to part 2 of *Crime and the Legal Process* (New York: McGraw-Hill, 1969).

18. Stephen R. Bing and S. Stephen Rosenfeld, *The Quality of Justice in the Lower Criminal Courts of Metropolitan Boston.* Report by Lawyer's Committee for Civil Rights under Law to the Governor's Commission on Law Enforcement and the Administration of Justice, 1980.

19. David Landy and Elliot Aronson, "The Influence of the Character of the Criminal and His Victim on the Decisions of Simulated Jurors," *Journal of Experimental Social Psychology* 5 (1969):141–152.

20. Michael G. Efran, "The Effect of Physical Appearance on the Judgment of Guilt, Interpersonal Attraction, and Severity of Recommended Punishment in a Simulated Jury Task," *Journal of Research in Personality* 8 (1974):45–54.

21. Karen K. Dion, "Physical Attractiveness and Evaluation of Children's Transgressions," *Journal of Personality and Social Psychology* 24 (1972):207–213.

22. W. N. Brooks and A. N. Doob, "Justice and the Jury," *Journal of Social Issues* 31 (1975):171–182.

23. Oliver Wendell Holmes, "Law in Science and Science in Law," *Harvard Law Review* 12 (1889):443; Roscoe Pound, "Law in Books and Law in Action," *American Law Review* 44 (1910):12.

24. Jerome Frank, *Law and the Modern Mind* (New York: Brentano's, 1936); and *Courts on Trial* (New York: Atheneum, 1949).

25. James Eisenstein and Herbert Jacob, *Felony Justice: An Organizational Analysis of Criminal Courts* (Boston: Little, Brown, and Co., 1977).

26. Ibid., p. 9.

Chapter 8

1. See, for example, statistics on arrests and case dispositions in Michael J. Hindelang, Michael R. Gottfredson, Christopher S. Dunn, and Nicollette Parisi, *Sourcebook of Criminal Justice Sta-*

tistics, 1976 (Albany, N.Y.: U.S. Department of Justice, Criminal Justice Research Center, 1977).

2. Jonathan D. Casper, *Criminal Courts: The Defendant's Perspective* (Washington, D.C.: U.S. Department of Justice, Government Printing Office, 1978), p. 14.

3. Howard S. Erlanger, "Jury Research in America: Its Past and Future," *Law and Society Review* 4 (February 1970):345–370.

4. William Labov, *Language in the Inner City* (Philadelphia: University of Pennsylvania Press, 1972).

5. Basil Bernstein, *Class, Codes, and Control* (New York: Schocken, 1971).

6. Maurice Bloch, "Introduction," in his *Political Language and Oratory in Modern Society* (New York: Academic Press, 1975).

7. For the development of this theme in various American political contexts, see Murray Edelman, *Political Language* (New York: Academic Press, 1977).

8. Daniel H. Swett, "Cultural Bias in the American Legal System," *Law and Society Review* 4 (August 1969):98.

9. John B. McConahay, Courtney J. Mullin, and Jeffrey Frederick, "The Uses of Social Science in Trials with Political and Racial Overtones: The Trial of Joan Little," *Law and Contemporary Problems* 41 (Winter 1977):212.

Index